A GILDED CAGE

Lucien Bonaparte
Prisoner of War 1810-1814

At Ludlow and Worcester

by

BARNEY ROLFE-SMITH

STONEBROOK PUBLISHING

A Gilded Cage

ISBN 978-0-9568972-2-0

First published in 2012 by Stonebrook Publishing, Stonebrook House Downton on the Rock, Ludlow, SY8 2LH.

Printed by Orphans Press, Leominster.

Publications by the same author:

Notes on Bringewood Forge and the Downton Walks, 2009, ISBN 0-954-31947-8

Fishing in Time, The History of the Leintwardine Fishing Club, 2011, ISBN 978-0-9568972-0-6

CONTENTS

MAPS, FAMILY TREES, ILLUSTRATIONS AND COLOUR PLATES

COLOUR PLATES

6

LUCIEN BONAPARTE'S EUROPE

<u>KEY</u>

1. Canino. 2. Civitavecchia. 3. Exeter. 4. Gloucester.

ITALY

Scale

0   100   200 Kms

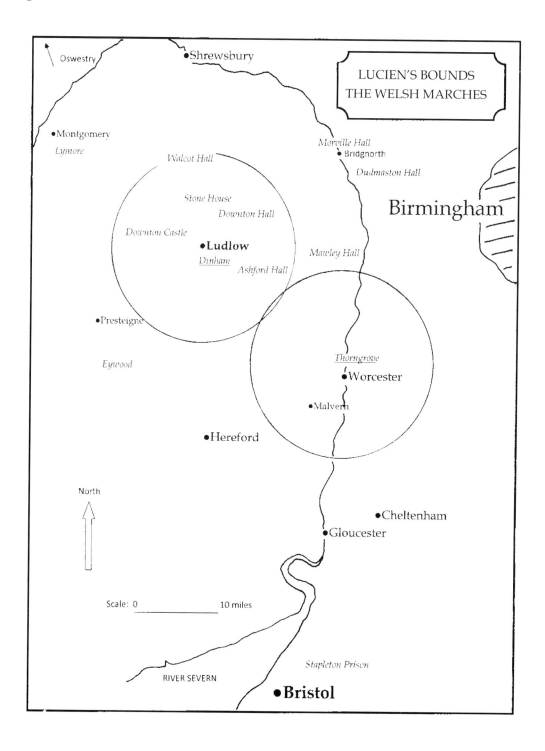

Oswestry

●Shrewsbury

LUCIEN'S BOUNDS
THE WELSH MARCHES

●Montgomery
Lymore

Moreville Hall
● Bridgnorth

Walcot Hall

Dudmaston Hall

Stone House
Downton Hall

Birmingham

Downton Castle

●**Ludlow**
Dinham

Mawley Hall

Ashford Hall

●Presteigne

Thorngrove

Eywood

●Worcester

●Malvern

●Hereford

North

●Cheltenham

●Gloucester

Scale: 0   10 miles

Stapleton Prison

RIVER SEVERN

●**Bristol**

This book is dedicated to Janet

Lucien Bonaparte
by François-Xavier Fabre and probably completed between 1808 and 1810.

Image courtesy of the Museo Napoleonico, Rome

A NOTE TO THE READER

Several short, and sometimes contradictory, literary references to the fact that Napoleon Bonaparte's brother had resided in Ludlow in 1811 sparked my desire to know more and ultimately to put the record straight. It was intriguing. England was at war with France and under threat of invasion by the Napoleonic armies. To the English people Napoleon embodied all that was considered evil; he was called 'The GREAT TYRANT'. He was the implacable enemy and yet Lucien Bonaparte, a Frenchman and brother of the enemy's leader, was not only allowed to live here in the heart of England but also to bring his wife, children and servants. How could this be? Was he a prisoner or guest? Where did he live? What did he do?

It was not a simple matter to find out. There are two versions of Lucien's *Memoirs* but they contain few details of his time in England.[1] Other biographers have chosen to skip over what turns out to have been a residency of some three and half years. Surely this was a long enough period of time for an imprint of his visit to register? Fortunately two hundred years ago the people of England were just as keen to find out why this family was here and what they got up to. The newspaper editors of the day were only too glad to supply the detail. Many of these newspapers, not easily accessible before now, have in 2012 been made available in a digitized format and this information, in addition to a detailed examination of the manuscript records held in the National Archives, has allowed me to turn the spotlight of history on to the circumstances surrounding this event and to set out this record.[2]

It is hoped the results of this research will help to add to the knowledge of life and attitudes in England during the late Georgian period and in particular in those places where Lucien was resident. There are several areas of interest. A more modern analogy might be to imagine the reaction and interest if Hitler's brother had come to live in England with his family during World War II. We will learn that the 'celebrity culture' is not a new phenomenon but one that was already well developed and that the attempted manipulation of public attitudes by the authorities and individuals using the medium of the 'press' was a regular occurrence. We are reminded that despite the absence of modern 'conveniences' such as computers and combustion engines, telephones and television, with determination life could be and was conducted very fully and with remarkable speed. Perhaps there are lessons we could learn from the civilized behavior shown by individuals to one another despite their nations being at war. In contrast we are reminded of the callousness and downright cruelty with which the under-privileged were treated and that but for the excesses of revolution in France, England may well have lost its own monarchy and a strata of its privileged elite. There is throughout this story the theme of a family unit beset by the vagaries of life in the early days of the 19th Century. Not an ordinary family but one that had experienced not only extraordinary privileges but also known utter despair. The resilience of this family and its determination to maintain its own set of values is remarkable.

By way of a short introduction to the story the reader should understand that Lucien Bonaparte came from a large family; he was the third eldest of eight children. In 1810 he was 35. He had already married for the second time and was caring for seven children. From childhood Lucien and Napoleon, who was the elder by six years, were often at odds. He initially supported his brother and had been instrumental in Napoleon's rise to power. However, he became increasingly unhappy with his elder brother's Imperial designs and by 1804 had given up any pretensions to be of assistance to Napoleon. Napoleon in his turn was wholly disenchanted with Lucien's attitude, and even his choice of wives; he continually demanded that Lucien divorce his second wife. Napoleon was angered and mystified by Lucien's refusal to take part in his Imperial schemes to retain power and influence in the hands of the Bonaparte family. He acknowledged Lucien's capabilities but distrusted his political ideas and even came to suspect that Lucien was actively working against him. Lucien, unwilling to compromise his ideals or his marriage, took up his brother's suggestion to move to Rome to keep out of the way. A few years later Lucien left Rome for the countryside. He hoped he could live quietly at Canino some ninety miles to the north of Rome in Tuscania, just south of the modern province of Tuscany. It was not to be. Almost by mutual consent of the Bonaparte family it was considered appropriate that Lucien and his family should emigrate to the United States of America.

CHAPTER ONE: THE CAPTURE

In 1810 Lucien Bonaparte and his family lived at Musignano a country house some 90 miles north-west of Rome, and just south of the small town of Canino. When the day came in August of that year to leave their home and set out to board ship for America there must have been a general feeling of trepidation and mixed emotions.[3] This departure had taken months of planning and preparation by both family and staff. They had all enjoyed a comfortable home in the countryside of Tuscania and relished the pleasant lifestyle.[4] Now they all were about to make a huge leap into the unknown.

Lucien had been contemplating emigration to America for some time but had always hoped that it could be avoided. If only 'they', the family, would leave him alone. Yet he knew he had little choice; he believed that his brother, who was becoming increasingly autocratic, was more than capable of having him arrested and even assassinated. Now that his mentor, his Holiness Pope Pius VII, had been obliged by Napoleon to go into exile in France, it seemed that there was now all the more reason to go. The main task was to get away and hope that his 'escape' would remain undetected until he was well beyond the influence of his 'imperial' brother, who he feared could change his mind at any time.

Alexandrine, Lucien's wife, would have shared his concerns but she would have been even more anxious for their children – aware of the risks and uncertainties of sailing across oceans but probably more concerned for their future as émigrés in a strange land far from the culture they had known.[5] For the thirty or so staff and servants accompanying them it was an act of faith that the head of the household knew what he was doing. Many of them had already followed him to Spain and to Paris and more recently here to Rome and Canino. Their loyalty was well proven but this voyage to the New World was a huge step. Was it a step too far? Perhaps some of the staff saw this as an opportunity for themselves in the 'land of the free'? In any event the decision had been made – it was time to depart.

In all probability Lucien, his secretary Monsieur Joseph Servières and his long time friend and companion Monsieur Count Charles de Châtillon had already set off for the port of Civitavecchia; the ancient port on Italy's east coast that served Rome.[6] If they were going to avoid last minute problems they needed to ensure that the family entourage could embark in suitable conditions and that the considerable baggage train, already on its way, was received aboard ship. The farewells from the old and infirm retainers remaining behind would have been loud and tearful as the convoy set off. The family would have been split between several coaches perhaps each holding an adult with one or two children. We might imagine that Alexandrine travelled with her youngest child the eighteen month old Paul[7] and his nurse-maid together with the family priest Père Maurice[8] as companion. In the next coach three year old Jeanne and her nursemaid travelled under the watchful eye of twelve year old Anna[9], Alexandrine's daughter from her first marriage, and perhaps accompanied by the family physician, Henri de France. Following on in the third was Lucien's nephew-by-marriage, André Boyer looking after Charlotte[10] or 'Lolotte' as the family called her and Christine-Egypta[11] known as 'Lili', the two girls, 15 and 12, were born to Lucien's first wife, Christine.[12] In the fourth coach, on one bench seat were Alexandrine's eldest Bonaparte children, Charles-Lucien, 7, and Letitia, 6 with their tutor, L'Abbé Charpentier de Bâle, on the other. Finally Madame Servières, the secretary's wife, and her child probably shared a carriage with some of the senior staff who, by one account, numbered 23 servants, ten women and thirteen men.[13] Some of these servants were Corsicans who had loyally followed Lucien from their homes in Ajaccio. Even if some of the younger servants had travelled both on top and behind each coach one could again imagine that two further coaches, or perhaps carts, would be needed to transport the remainder of the retinue.

After the farewells the bone shaking tedium of the 40 mile journey would have soon taken its toll on everyone's patience as the carriages creaked and groaned on the hot dusty road to Civitavecchia. Given the young age of the children and the slowness of travelling in convoy on poor roads they may well have had a night's rest on the way. The sight of the sea and the tangle of ships' masts would have raised their spirits and signalled a welcome relief to the end of the first phase of their journey. As they approached closer to the quay that lay under the protection of the round turrets of Fort Michelangelo they would have seen their ship anchored a few hundred yards offshore identified by its American flag hanging limply from the stern post. As their cutter approached the ship its name would have been discernible on the stern, *Hercules*.

The story of how this American vessel, *Hercules*, came to be chosen is an interesting one and comes from the detail gleaned from the subsequent legal action taken by the crew.[14] They were to sue the owner, in a Massachusetts court, for the wages that they were owed from this voyage. It would appear that due to the risks of sailing into the European war zone the owners had intended only paying wages if the voyage made a profit. It would seem that this condition had not been explained to the crew when the *Hercules,* under the command of its master Edward West, had sailed from Salem, America, on 2 August 1809. The ship arrived at her Naples destination on 15 September where she unloaded her cargo only to find as it was taken ashore that it had been sequestered by the Neapolitan Government and auctioned off. Then in March 1810 the *Hercules* and her crew, which had been detained for the past four months at Naples, learned that, along with 29 other American vessels, it had been confiscated. This order had been made apparently by the then King of Naples and Sicily, Joachim-Napoleon Murat (Lucien's brother-in-law) on orders 'from Paris' for violating the blockade.[15] The ships and their cargoes were then to be sold off and the proceeds used by the government. Edward West and his crew remained aboard, prisoners in their own ship. West could only sit and wait for his ship to suffer a similar fate to those others that had already been sold. He started to seek a way out of his predicament by trying to find a buyer for the vessel and ideally one who would then be prepared to hire him to sail it. Then to his great surprise and delight a 'high ranking official' came aboard and offered to return the *Hercules* and his ship's papers, as well as repay the expenses of his lost cargo, which was worth, it was understood, more than $60,000. All he had to do was to sail to Civitavecchia and take on freight for Philadelphia. Despite his ready agreement he was escorted there by the corvette *Achille*, they arrived at Civitavecchia on 21 July. It was only then that he found out that the 'freight' included a human element. He was to take Lucien, his family, staff and freight directly to America. For this service he received a $2000 advance with a promise of $8000 more if he safely delivered his passengers and cargo to Philadelphia.

Edward West must have been a happy man not only to be set free and have his cargo paid for but also to be given fare-paying passengers for the return voyage home. However, to accommodate some forty extra people, particularly as many were women and children, for a voyage that would last several weeks, was a challenge.[16] He was helped by the line of credit that had been given to him by the same official to fit the ship out. He set his crew to work. The carpenters would have been kept very busy creating extra cabins and sleeping spaces. No doubt West would have felt obliged to give up his cabin to this noble visitor and his wife but under the circumstances be happy to do so. With the preparations complete he would have welcomed the family aboard and introduced them to their new surroundings in good humour. After a few last minute purchases of extra rations and other comforts; the *Hercules* set sail on 8 August despite a rising wind and a falling barometer reading.[17] Lucien was keen to go and would not hear of any delay.

Once under way and with the family settled into some sort of routine Lucien would have had some time to reflect. He made a mental note to thank his sister, Caroline Murat, for her assistance in persuading her husband to take the risk of helping him to the extent that he had. The unresolved problem that still remained was getting past the British. His request for Mr Hill, Britain's

Minister to the King of Sardinia at Cagliari, to provide him with safe passage had not arrived.[18] Lucien had no option but to accept the risk and hope they would get past the British undetected. Perhaps the poor weather would help cover their escape.

It was not long before this same poor weather became a hindrance rather than a help. Many of the passengers were seriously seasick. Either Captain West, or the state of the family, persuaded Lucien it was foolish to go on and the *Hercules* sought shelter in the Bay of Cagliari, at the southern end of the island of Sardinia, and anchored there in the 'Roads' on 10 August. Lucien was keen to get his family ashore and sent messages to the Sardinian King, Victor Emanuel I, asking for permission to land. Lucien now encountered his next problem. Victor Emanuel I had been obliged to flee Italy for Sardinia when he inherited the Savoy crown in 1802 and subsequently set up his government at Cagliari. He had no love for the French. Lucien would have known that the King of Sardinia was allied with England and would have preferred to have avoided all contact with both Sardinia and the British but now he had no option but to fall upon their mercy.

Lucien asked Mr Hill, who was still at Cagliari, to support this request. He was after all the same man to whom he had applied successfully for a passport two years before. Mr Hill saw matters differently. He was there to maintain a friendly relationship with the Savoy government and to see that England's interests were upheld by advising them appropriately. Hill felt he could not help and his advice to the Savoy government was to allow Lucien to tie up alongside the quarantine quarters, an isolation area, probably a ship's hulk in the bay, in which they would be confined. Lucien pleaded by letter to the King; according to *ses Mémoires*, he wrote seventeen letters between 10 and 20 August. He even wrote several times to the Russian ambassador, Prince Koslovski and asked him to help but received the reply that as Russia was currently Napoleon's ally he could only oppose the request.[19] During the period that these negotiations took place another British ship arrived at Cagliari on 14 August, HMS *Salsette*.[20]   It happened that Sir Robert Adair was on board.[21] He was recently Ambassador to the Porte (Turkish Empire) and, due to ill-health, was on his way back to England. The ship may well have been calling in at Cagliari to pick up dispatches or was forced there by the same storm that Lucien encountered. Mr Hill and Sir Robert discussed the situation. Mr Hill then directed[22] that Sir Robert was to seek an interview with Lucien and inform him 'that there was no chance of his being allowed to go to America'. The meeting took place apparently at the 'Health Station', as the ship or hulk used as the quarantine quarters was known.

Lucien continued to plead his case and asked that his family be permitted to go ashore if he agreed to stay on board. Mr Hill must have been instrumental in advising the King to refuse permission. The King took his advice and additionally asked Lucien to leave his bay. In a subsequent conversation Lucien asked Sir Robert if he might sail in convoy with him in the *Hercules* when he returned to England but was told 'that, even if that request was granted, he could not answer for his being allowed to remain on English ground except as a prisoner of war'. Lucien then asked to be allowed either to remain in Sardinia or return to Civitavecchia but, according to the (British) Cabinet Memorandum on Lucien's arrest, Mr Hill decided that 'the most prudent course would be to conduct him to Malta; there to await the decision of His Majesty's Government'.[23] After some hesitation Lucien apparently acquiesced to this plan to be taken to Malta as a prisoner of war. It is most likely that Sir Robert informed Lucien that he should surrender to HMS *Pomone*, a frigate already in the area and which may already have been in the bay. At this point, having given his instructions to Captain Robert Barrie of *Pomone*, Sir Robert did not stay to see what would occur but left to continue his journey to England on 16 August.[24] No doubt he wished to report as quickly as possible the news that Mr Hill had ordered Captain Barrie to take the *Hercules* and convey the prisoners to Malta where they could be held until it was decided what to do with them.

Lucien on the eve of his departure from Cagliari received a note from the Sardinian Court that infuriated him. It implied that he had agreed to become a prisoner of war. He wrote at once to Mr Hill and protested that he had not willingly given himself up as a prisoner and protested that the court had been wrongly informed. He complained that he had not been allowed to go to England, or to return to Civitavecchia or even remain in Sardinia and that if he left the harbour he would be stopped and taken to Malta. He protested again that having sought passports he could not be considered a prisoner of war. It was a muddled argument that held no water. It was quite clear, and he knew it, that once he set out from the bay at Cagliari he would be stopped and arrested. Those were the instructions to Captain Barrie and so on 20 August when *Hercules* set sail it was apprehended once out of sight of land by Barrie who then demanded Lucien's surrender.

Mr Hill later observed that it did not really matter if Lucien had properly understood that he was to be a prisoner or not as 'it certainly did not entirely depend upon his will whether he wished to capitulate, or surrender at discretion'. The fact of the matter was that he was not going anywhere on his own. The *Pomone* was a 38 gun frigate and under her Captain had had a very successful war and he and her crew were a very experienced and a very efficient fighting unit.[25] There was no question of trying to avoid capture. The *Hercules* had no option but to 'heave to'. According to Lucien's *Memoirs* a junior British officer came aboard and having established that he was indeed addressing Lucien Bonaparte and not Signor Fabricio (one of Lucien's aliases) asked, apparently rather brusquely, whether he wished to be taken to England or Malta;

(we know that the *Memoirs* are in error here as there was no choice of destination offered). The officer apparently returned to his ship and then brought back Captain Barrie's invitation for Lucien and his family to join him (presumably accompanied by only a few servants) on board *Pomone* for the passage. A British crew was put aboard the *Hercules* and both ships set sail in convoy for Malta.

According to the *Memoirs*, and this is probably an accurate observation this time, Captain Barrie's 'attentions during the passage, were infinite, and marked by the most refined delicacy'. Later the British newspapers reported that the captain and crew, who were entitled to share the prize money that would normally be offered by the Navy for any ships captured, had followed their captain's lead and, so the story went, had declined to take the prize money as they gallantly declared they had not fought for their prize and so did not feel entitled to accept the reward.[26] Lucien apparently tried to reward them with cash for allowing him to keep his luggage but this too was refused. Alexandrine's gift of several gallons of beer was apparently duly and gratefully accepted. It is possible that having so many pretty ladies on board might have had a civilizing effect on these hardened naval warriors but it is rather more likely that none of the crew would openly question their captain.

Their arrival in Malta less than a week later on 24 August took the British Governor, Lieutenant General Sir Hildebrand Oakes, by surprise. Having spoken to Captain Barrie on board *Pomone* General Oakes immediately sent a dispatch to the Secretary of State for War and the Colonies, the Earl of Liverpool, stating his objections to the idea of allowing Lucien to come ashore at Malta. He spoke to Lucien and informed him that he and his family were now prisoners of war. Lucien asked to put his family ashore and after some deliberation with his colleagues the General reluctantly agreed that they could come ashore but then chose the most secure accommodation at his disposal in which to put them; Fort Ricasoli. This bleak and cheerless fort at the entrance to the harbour, baking in the summer heat, was not in the best of condition. Three years before mutineers from Frobert's Regiment had objected to the treatment given to them by their mainly German officers and had seized the fort.[27] Although most of the mutineers were captured a small party seized the explosives magazine in the fort and attempted to bargain for their freedom. Negotiations failed and the mutineers blew up the store destroying much of the fort. It was into these ruins, presumably patched up to some extent, that the Governor of Malta put Lucien and his family. The *Memoir* describes the governor as a 'rigid character' but that despite the situation he treated Lucien with 'deference and politeness'. Nevertheless the General was not prepared to allow Lucien or his family out of the fort and demanded to have sight of any letters that Lucien wished to send or receive. There was no doubt in the General's mind that he was dealing with prisoners of war and until he heard differently that was how he would treat them.

CHAPTER TWO: REFLECTIONS

Exactly where Lucien would have had his rooms in Fort Ricasoli is unclear but it takes little imagination to picture the images of despair that Lucien and his family must have made as they considered the prospect of living in this forbidding place. The circumstances could not have been worse. They could not go on and they could not go back. Hardly a month earlier they had been in their own home and able to look down on their cattle grazing on the lush fields of their estate and perhaps contemplate a swim in the cool stream. Now all they could do was retreat into the shadows of the fort to escape the blistering heat outside. Perhaps Lucien sought further escape from whimpering children and whining staff and found a room where he could be alone to think and plan a way out of this hell.

A westerly facing window would have allowed Lucien to look out to the sea and the direction he so desperately wanted to take through the Straits of Gibraltar, into the Atlantic and on to America. He must have reflected on all that had gone before. What could he have done differently? Was there a chance the British would let him go? Even if he got back to Musignano, could he live there? He knew the answer – his brother was never going to let him rest. How had it come to this? He acknowledged that even when briefly at the same school in the south of France they had never got along. Even at the Battle of Toulon, Napoleon at the age of 24, commanding the artillery, had ordered him off the field of battle as being no fit place for him. Lucien knew also that his first marriage, to his lovely Christine (page 71), had upset the family. The innkeeper's daughter was not deemed suitable. He had only one regret however – that she had died so young. Their children, Lolotte and Lili, were a permanent reminder of the love they shared. Josephine, Napoleon's wife, had never liked Christine and had been particularly spiteful to her which no doubt reflected Napoleon's attitude. Lucien had accepted several boring jobs that Napoleon had arranged for him; such as the one in Antwerp, and he again acknowledged to himself that walking out after six weeks had not helped his cause.[28] His election to the Council of Five Hundred and his subsequent elevation as its President was something that he could be proud of; it was after all his intervention that had provided the catalyst for Napoleon to become First Consul of France. He was particularly proud of his later work as Minister for the Interior. He had enjoyed much of the job and had demonstrated a real talent for building public art collections. Yet again he acknowledged to himself that his grasp of running the department had been lax and many, including Napoleon, complained of his failure to oversee his officials and rein in their corruption.

The fact was that when Christine died in May of 1800 his world had fallen apart. Lucien had left the running of the Ministry to others. The reports against him and his growing wish for a revolutionary but representative government only served to alienate Napoleon further who now thought Lucien far too Jacobin (left-wing). Even his work in his next role as Ambassador to the Spanish Court in Madrid did not meet with approval. His assignment was to persuade Spain to attack Portugal in order to deny the British access to the Portuguese ports. A short and limited campaign resulted in the Treaty of Badajoz; peace between the two nations. This was not exactly what Napoleon intended; he had hoped for a war to crush Portugal. He refused to ratify the treaty at first and kept his army in Spain. Lucien saw this as risking war with Spain and objected fiercely to his brother's attitude. He considered his task complete and asked to return to France but was refused. By the time Lucien had made up his mind to resign his post and return to Paris he had at least improved his own financial position. He had managed to add significantly to his growing art collection and he had been 'gifted' a quantity of uncut diamonds worth several million francs from the governments of both Spain and Portugal for brokering the peace. Thus on his return to Paris at the end of 1801 as a private citizen and without paid employment he could afford to live without an appointment for a while. His return did nothing to improve the relationship with Napoleon and there was no reconciliation.

Lucien was therefore surprised when he was appointed to the Senate and considered that it was probably an attempt by Napoleon to keep him out of active politics but still in a position to oblige his loyalty. Lucien accepted the job for the prosaic reason that it provided a good salary. The relationship between the brothers might have settled down at this point had not Lucien met Madame Alexandrine Jouberthon, a married woman, and had fallen in love. Her husband, Gian Francesco Ippolito Jouberthon de Vamberthy was abroad in Saint-Domingue, then a French Colony on the Caribbean island of Hispaniola, where he was working to pay off his debtors. The unfortunate man did not suffer long as he died of a fever shortly after his arrival. Lucien and Alexandrine were not free to marry however, as a death certificate was required in addition to the normal widow's conventions of waiting for the mourning period to be over. Their relationship was well known in society and the rumours abounded that they were indeed already married. Lucien denied these rumours not wishing to provoke Napoleon, who had intended that Lucien should marry the recently widowed Queen of Etruria. Alexandrine, and her daughter, Anna, were installed by Lucien in a house close to his own (reportedly connected by a secret tunnel). Lucien continued to argue with his brother for his independence but Napoleon's only response was to place a secret police watch on Lucien's activities.

Lucien's tunnel must have been used well. The police did not manage to impede the love affair and Alexandrine gave birth to their first child, Charles, in May 1803. A civil marriage ceremony took place in the following October, conducted quietly on Lucien's country estate, Le Plessis Chamant, witnessed only by local people. Lucien duly informed his brother of what he had done. Napoleon was outraged and refused to recognize the marriage. He demanded that the couple divorce and, illogically, at the same time declared the marriage invalid. Napoleon, perhaps influenced by his mother, Letizia, and Caroline, his sister, sought a way out of this predicament for Lucien. He wrote to the Pope, Pope Pius VII, and asked that he invite Lucien to study antiquities in Rome. By Easter 1804, Lucien, his wife, and their combined family of three daughters and one son had left Paris for Italy. A few weeks later Napoleon declared himself Emperor and announced that Lucien and his family would be excluded from any succession rights.

Once in Rome Lucien, who had acquired the spacious mansion Palazzo Nuñez, started to settle his family and his growing picture collection into their new home. This commitment to accommodating his household in Rome had the added benefit of strengthening Lucien's friendship with the Pope and for a year or two life at the Palazzo must have been both secure and pleasant.

Throughout 1806 Napoleon was occupied with advancing other members of his family and consolidating his power base; Joseph, the eldest of all the Bonaparte brothers, was appointed to the Kingdom of Naples and Louis, Lucien's junior by three years, to be King of Holland. Lucien wanted no part in his brother's empire and continued to seek the quiet life. He purchased a country house, the Villa Rufinella, just outside Rome in the pleasant hills of Frascati, for use in the summer and escape the heat of the city. Joseph continued to mediate between the two brothers and arranged for them to meet, with the hope that they might resolve their issues, but the central problem remained insurmountable – Lucien would not give up Alexandrine.

In 1807 Napoleon became increasingly irritated by the Pope who had permitted 'Christian' shipping, which included the British, to use papal ports and he subsequently ordered his troops to occupy Rome. Lucien publicly declared support for the Pope but soon felt obliged to leave Rome for his own safety. It was at this point, and to the mutual advantage of both Lucien and the Pope – who needed money – that Lucien bought the Canino estate, which included the Musignano property. Here, still within the Papal States, but not under direct French rule, he hoped to remain out of sight and provide a settled environment for Alexandrine to give birth to their fourth child, Paul. There was still the need to keep out of his brother's way as Lucien knew that Napoleon was writing to his brother Joseph in terms that made it clear that he saw Lucien as his enemy.

Lucien recalled how he was not allowed to disappear. Another offer from Napoleon arrived, again via Joseph, of various kingdoms that Napoleon was prepared to offer, but still on the proviso that he gave up Alexandrine. Lucien refused again and recognized that the pressure would remain unrelenting. It was then that he seriously contemplated emigration to America and even made contact with the nearest British Minister, at Cagliari, Sardinia, to sound out if he might be eligible for a safe passage across the seas; it appeared that the response was positive. However the lure of life on his estate held him back. He enjoyed the estate he had bought. He had developed an old convent that lay within it as his summer home. Musignano, as the house was called, was a favourite with the children as it gave them the freedom to roam the woods around and swim in the river and it allowed him to follow some of his own interests such as cotton growing and renovating an iron foundry. One can imagine how much he hoped that it would work out and he would not be forced to leave.

Throughout 1809 Lucien was under almost constant emotional blackmail by letter from his mother in Paris to send his eldest daughter, Charlotte, to her. The intention was to marry the 15 year old to the advantage of the family. Charlotte was desperately unhappy in Paris and begged to come home. Finally the Emperor himself had had enough of the situation and despite his mother's protests ordered Charlotte back to Italy and renewed the demand that Lucien either get divorced or set out for America. Lucien, angry in his turn at the treatment his daughter was getting, demanded that Charlotte be returned immediately. He told his brother that he had applied for safe passage and was now looking for a ship. Much to Lucien's relief, after three months separation, Charlotte returned to Canino in early June 1810. The passports from the French police had arrived at about the same time which meant that the only matter to stop the family from leaving had been the lack of a passport from the British.

A sudden breeze through the window brought him back to the present and his Maltese prison. Perhaps, he ruefully reflected, he should not have taken the risk of travelling without the passport. There was no use dwelling on the past - he needed to do something about making life more comfortable for his family. He sat down and wrote to General Oakes demanding better accommodation as he did not think he should be treated as a prisoner of war. Apparently nine letters in total were sent to the General's office over the next few days. Lucien even refused the General's invitation to dine arguing that he could not if he was considered a 'close prisoner'. Both the tone of his letters 'the particular haughtiness of expression' and Lucien's 'supercilious refusal' of the invitation only served to irritate the General.[29] Oakes had in fact already considered permitting Lucien to stay in his own house, St Antonio, as he knew he could keep his eye on the family there but now he was in no hurry to make the offer. However, he permitted some furniture to be brought over from Valetta and decided to wait until he was asked properly for better accommodation. The provision of some comforts was just as well as it was two weeks before the general considered that he had received a proper request. General Oakes permitted Lucien to move to into St Antonio on 12 September. This country house, that lay some five miles from Valetta, is described in Badger's book as being built for a former Grand Master, Grand Master de Paula, 'the situation being exceedingly pleasant, spacious and commodious'.[30] The apartments were mostly unfurnished, the General was a bachelor, and Lucien, confining himself to 'what was absolutely necessary', only bought furniture to the amount of 300 guineas. At last the family and particularly the young children began to enjoy life a little more. During the day Lucien resumed the composition of a poem he had started to write in Musignano, *Charlemagne*, but spent the evenings with the family which were taken up with music and dancing and the performance of plays.

General Oakes as one can see from his career record had spent most of his life fighting the French and although he treated Lucien 'with every respect' he was not going to take any chances.[31] Despite obtaining Lucien's parole he did not forget his responsibilities as gaoler. Lucien would remain guarded and escorted should he ever leave the house. Although he reduced the size of the guard to 21 soldiers the General still required two officers, Captain Marshall and Lieutenant Harold, to remain with the guard and ensure that nothing went awry.

As one can imagine Lucien's arrival on Malta would have caused quite a stir amongst the population and particularly the British on the island and whilst his letters were subject to censorship theirs were not. Within three weeks of his arrival and his imprisonment on Malta letters, and thus news of the event, had reached England through these informal channels. The exciting news spread rapidly.

CHAPTER THREE: UNDER ESCORT

In England the appetite for further news of Lucien's capture was growing. Newspapers throughout the kingdom started to brief their readership on Lucien's activities. The news was generally collated by editors using the letters from abroad that had been received by private individuals and then reported to the newspaper rather than from dedicated and trained correspondents as we would expect these days. Consequently many of the initial reports are contradictory or even totally wrong. The public at this time were quite used to this and had learned to 'read between the lines' and they knew that over time a more factual picture gradually emerged. For instance *The Morning Post*, a London paper, carried a rather muddled report on 4 October 1810 which confirmed the rumours already circulating that Lucien had left Italy but also that the reports of his capture were untrue and that he was now on his way to Gibraltar with Mr Hill's permission. On the same page was a letter from Gibraltar dated 7 September 1810 which reported accurately that the *Salsette* had just arrived with Mr Adair, Minister to the Porte, and that Mr Hill had in fact ordered that for 'the greater security of these voluntary exiles', they should be transported to Malta under convoy of the frigate *Pomone* to await the pleasure of government as to their future disposal. Incidentally, for those interested in the fate of the *Hercules*, news had reached Bristol by 2 October that the ship had now reached her home port at Salem.

The Morning Chronicle, another London paper, on 5 October, provided its readers with confirmation that Lucien had arrived in Malta and provided some background information as to why Lucien had taken this action. This information came from an unidentified correspondent from Malta written on the 25 August:

> LUCIEN BONAPARTE and his family, Madame B, seven children, and a retinue, altogether upwards of 40 persons, were brought here the 23rd inst by Captain BARRIE, in the Pomone frigate, who found them on board an American vessel, off Cagliari, in Sardinia, a few days back, where they had been 8 or 9 days, endeavoring to be allowed to land; but which they were peremptorily refused. It seems they embarked from Civitavecchia, in the Roman States, about three weeks ago. He gives out, that as he had refused to divorce his wife, become King of Rome, and marry his daughter (about 15

years old, and now here with the rest of his children) to FERDINAND VII of Spain, he has been exiled from the Continent of Europe, and that he intended proceeding to America. General OAKES waited on him yesterday after-noon, and informed him, that as he wished to land, he should be provided with accommodations in Fort Ricasoli, where both himself and family would be treated with every attention, but that, of course, he could not but be considered a prisoner of war. He is, we learn, to remain here until directions from Government at home shall be received about him.

The Morning Chronicle then provided its readers with some deeper back-ground material:

Bonaparte was extremely offended with Lucien for his marriage with his present wife, a Madame JAUBERTON [in fact Jouberthon], the widow of an Exchange-broker. The marriage took place just before Bonaparte usurped the Throne of France: as soon as the Tyrant heard of it, he said to LUCIEN, in a violent rage, "Comment vous savez ce qui passé maintenant et vous allez epouse un Catin." "Eh bien" replied Lucien, "elle est au moins jeune et jolie." This sneer, which was directed against JOSEPHINE, who was then in high favour, so enraged BONAPARTE, that he never saw LUCIEN afterwards. BONAPARTE has, however, repeatedly, since LUCIEN's residence at Rome, pressed him to be divorced from his wife, in order that he might contract a marriage more suitable to the Imperial Blood of the BONAPARTES; but LUCIEN, who is very much attached to her, has steadily refused to comply with this request. It is very likely that an apprehension that the Tyrant would take more effectual means to remove her, may have had a great influence on LUCIEN'S mind, and as Madame LUCIEN could not be without fears of the same kind, it is probable that her influence was exercised to induce her husband to remove beyond the power of his brother. Lucien acquired immense wealth while he was Ambassador in Spain, and it is generally understood, that when he negotiated the peace with Portugal, he obtained from the Portuguese Government a douceur of six million of livres, or about £280,000 sterling.

Further reports stated that the Portuguese Government did not have the cash to give him and so gave him the equivalent worth in rough diamonds. These were later purchased by Mr Salomons of London, a diamond merchant.

The provincial papers in England are quick to repeat the articles that the London Papers have published and add some more spicy information whenever they can: *The Hereford Journal* of 10 October showed a little more of the 'Malta' letter above and included what the letter refers to as 'garrison gossip' when referring to Lucien's daughter, Charlotte, who had been intended for Ferdinand: '[she] is a beautiful girl, and worthy a better fate. If reports speak true, there are those in the Garrison upon whom her black eyes have already had a deadly influence … . The curiosity that they excite, may more easily be imagined than described.' Even descriptions of Lucien were now being circulated: 'He is a man of about five feet three or four inches high, and of a severe and melancholy aspect.'

Thus we can see that the excitement was mounting and that it was almost expected that the prisoners would be brought to England – and what a snub that would be to the 'TYRANT!' Some commentators however, were already displeased with the attitude the press was taking to this Frenchman believing that most of what had been heard about Lucien's motives for leaving Italy was false. One William Cobbett comments on the Bonaparte brothers' relationship:

> It seldom happens that wicked men can put faith in each other. A robber is extremely suspicious of his comrade, if he thinks him to be as arrant a rogue as himself. This remark will apply to the distrust and jealousy harboured by Napoleon against Lucien; who though as vicious as his brother in every respect, is more calm, more tranquil, more premeditated, is of a less turbulent temper, and has not the degree of insanity about him which his brother has. In private life, Lucien is as bad as Napoleon; in the political he is not so dangerous, because he is not a military man. Napoleon well knows that Lucien is a man of considerable talents, has read much, and has cultivated his mind. He appears affable, and has a great deal of "suaviter in modo".

Throughout this period instructions were being requested by General Oakes from the British government and they in their turn needed more detail of Lucien's intentions. As the weeks went by Lucien must have become increasingly irritated at the delay in deciding his future. One reason for this delay was that the Secretary of State for Foreign Affairs, the Marquess Wellesley was concerned about legality of arresting Lucien.[32] He requested that the King's Advocate provide an opinion 'whether or no' the 'government 'was entitled by the laws of nations to consider Lucien Bonaparte as a prisoner of war'. C H R Robinson, King's Advocate, was humbly of the opinion that the government *was* so entitled. On the same day that this opinion was delivered, 15 October 1810, instructions were sent to Malta, including a letter from the Marquess which informed Lucien that His Majesty 'could not permit him either to repair to America, or to remain in the Island of Malta: but that His Majesty was disposed to afford to him and his family an asylum in England upon his parole, and under such regulations as the peculiar nature of his situation would appear to require.'

The British Admiralty, having received the Secretary of State's subsequent request that they send a vessel to collect the brother of the Emperor, and their implacable enemy, must have sucked their teeth. One could imagine the old Admiral's comments: they were trying to fight a war for God's sake! To fit out a warship to receive 40 or so civilian French and Italian passengers and many tons of freight and then send it to the Mediterranean and back was no small task, it was not as if they could be packed into the space on the gun decks like soldiers!

Their Lordships would of course carry out the request but we could speculate that they reserved the right to indulge in a little irony. Of all the ships at their disposal they chose to send HMS *President*.[33] This 40 gun frigate had been captured from the French just four years before in the Bay of Biscay. Commissioned by the French navy in 1804 as the *Président* she was well regarded by each navy as a fast and well built vessel (she later served as a model for several future British builds). Having been converted for British service after her capture she was sent to South American waters. In 1810 she was about to depart for the Far East under Captain Samuel Warren when this new task was given to her.[34] He set sail for the Mediterranean as soon as he could.

Meanwhile on Malta General Oakes was getting increasingly concerned at Lucien's activities and he wrote, on 16 November, a private and confidential letter to Lord Liverpool, who was then the Secretary of State for War and the Colonies, and explained his earlier reasons for his recommendation for not permitting Lucien to remain on the island. He described:

> having the strongest reason to suspect, amounting almost to proof, that Lucien Bonaparte notwithstanding his Parole of Honor to communicate in writing to no one without my knowledge, has been carrying on a clandestine correspondence with Her Sicilian Majesty by means of emissaries sent for the purpose from Palermo, on the subject of a loan she wished to obtain from him, or to effect through his medium at Vienna. [He goes on to describe the involvement of several other persons

including a 'Spanish lady' in the plot and ends by saying] .. I have conceived it highly necessary that they [Lucien et al] should be got rid of as soon as possible. [A final paragraph] .. I am happy to say they embark this day, and I hope the *President* will sail in the evening.

We know from the log of HMS *President* that by 6 November Captain Warren was in Valletta harbour re-supplying his ship and making repairs. He took Lucien and the family on board on the 16th and no doubt General Oakes heaved a sigh of relief as the cutter took Lucien and his family off his island to become someone else's responsibility. HMS *President* finally headed away under full sail for England on the 17th. Other reports which indicated that she did not leave Malta until 29 November are incorrect.

The winter weather was not kind to the passengers and crew. Mercifully the ship made a fast passage and the agony of sea sickness for the family was not prolonged. On 3 December they passed by the Rock of Gibraltar. As they approached Lizard Point the weather must have improved as it was possible to enjoy a game of backgammon, as Charles de Châtillon's sketch of some of the family shows (page 72/73). The Lizard was sighted on Thursday 13 December 1810 and by that afternoon they had arrived off Plymouth, on the south-west coast of England [35] At last the English press were able to obtain some eyewitness accounts rather than relying on hearsay. *The Morning Post* was quick to report a letter:

> From Plymouth, 13 December. This morning arrived the President frigate, of 38 Guns, Captain Warren, from Malta, last from Gibraltar, having on board LUCIEN BONAPARTE and suite, consisting of near thirty persons. On her coming to anchor, she was put under quarantine, so we can obtain no particulars. – This afternoon Captain Nash, of the Salvador del Mundo, went alongside the President, and took with him some fish, oysters, and a variety of vegetables, as a present to Madame LUCIEN BONAPARTE and family. Should the weather permit the telegraph to work to and from London, we may expect his coming on shore. He is rather tall and thin, and at a small distance from the boat alongside, appears about thirty-five years of age. He does not speak a word of English.[36]

The Times, 19 December, repeated much of the same detail but informed us that as the *President* was anchored in Plymouth Sound and as the wind was fresh with a heavy swell Lucien had requested the *President* be allowed to move to smoother waters as his wife was 'extremely ill' and had been throughout the voyage. The paper went on to describe Lucien as 'a fine looking man, but appears very much in dudgeon at his detention. He has brought considerable property with him.'

In the same paper the editor chose to express what he must have felt was the mood of his readers concerning 'not one of the least remarkable occurrences of the present eventful times'. He wrote:

> We know not what may be the intention of our Govern-
> ment with respect to LUCIEN and his family; but at the
> same time that we wish him to be treated with courtesy
> and indulgence, we trust that all possible care will be
> taken to render harmless his residence among us. The
> unprecedented number of foreigners that are now resid-
> ing in this country under various pretexts, is certainly
> calculated to excite jealousy and suspicion: and the
> principles of LUCIEN are too well known to admit a
> doubt that all due precautions will be resorted to in
> respect to him.

Lucien may well have been in 'dudgeon' at having to remain on board for quarantine purposes but that requirement applied to any ship arriving at an English port. At least they had received some fresh food. It would have been appreciated that Captain Warren could have done little to influence these matters and that he continued to do what he could to make them comfortable. A later report suggested that Lucien's request to move to calmer waters had been met and the *President* had moved to Barnpool which offered good shelter.[37] Here Lucien amused himself sketching 'the beautiful seat of Lord Mount Edgcumbe.' The paper also reported that on the night before Lucien came ashore 'there was a grand ball aboard the President, which was attended by several naval officers, with their wives and daughters.' One could imagine that it was at this event that Lucien reportedly presented Captain Warren with a diamond studded gold watch in thanks for the consideration the ship and its crew had given to Lucien and his family.[38] Lucien's *Memoir* also states that Captain Warren, in return for the watch he received, presented Lucien with a 'beautiful' double-barrelled shotgun. It is hard to imagine that the good captain had anticipated this exchange of gifts and presumably had to send ashore for the best that Plymouth had to offer. Alternatively it may have been his own gun – in any event it reportedly became Lucien's favourite fowling piece during his stay in England.

Although Lucien was no doubt flattered by all this attention he must have had many questions about the details of his detention which had not yet been explained to him. He very much wanted to have a reply to the letter he had sent the moment of his arrival off Plymouth. Uppermost in his mind would have been the urgent need to get his family ashore as they were all sick – literally – and tired of being tossed around on board ship and of being cold and damp. It seemed he got his wish as the following letter of response shows:

> M Lucien Bonaparte
>
> Foreign Office   December 15th 1810
>
> I have had the honour to receive your letter dated from Plymouth the 13th instant, and I learn with great satisfaction, that your accommodation on board His Majesty's Ship has been agreeable to your wishes.
>
> Orders will be issued this day from the Admiralty for permitting you to land with your family and suite. A gentleman who I have appointed to meet you at Plymouth for the purpose of facilitating such arrangements as may be necessary for your establishment on shore will be authorized to communicate with you on all the details of that subject.
>
> The necessary orders will be given for landing your effects, subject only to the Regulations of the Custom House.
>
> I shall be happy to avail myself of any opportunity which may occur, of rendering your establishment convenient to yourself and to your family.
>
> I have the Honor (sic) to be, Sir, Your most obedient & humble Servant
>
> (signed) Wellesley

By Wednesday 19 December the London press, but probably not Lucien, knew that:[39]

> it is finally determined … LUCIEN BONAPARTE will take up his residency in Montgomeryshire. Government has sent … Mr Mackenzie … who was acquainted with Lucien, at Rome, some years ago [re an exchange of prisoners] to accompany him to his new residence. Three or four places, among others Ludlow, had been thought of to submit to him for his election; but on inquiry none

of them were found to contain a house fit and ready for the reception of so large an establishment. This difficulty being known, Earl Powis very politely offered, through Government, his seat of Linures [The press got the name wrong- it is Lymore] in Montgomeryshire, which has been accepted. It is an ancient castle [in fact, a 'black and white' house], with a large park, and ample pleasure grounds, situated in a beautiful part of the country, and affording every facility for the sports of the field. .. it will, no doubt, prove highly acceptable to a man of Lucien's taste.[40]

We find out later that Lymore was already being used to house a number of French officer prisoners of war on parole and these had been moved out and sent to Brecon, in south Wales.[41] The papers had correctly reported that it was the same Mr Mackenzie that had been sent across the Channel but in fact he had been sent to Morlaix, in Brittany, earlier that year to negotiate a prisoner exchange (which did not work out) there is no record of Lucien and Mackenzie meeting in Rome as the papers stated. We could presume therefore that Mackenzie may well have spoken fluent French.

It has not been satisfactorily explained why this part of England had been chosen to house Lucien. Some accounts have suggested that he was able to choose his place of imprisonment but this was not so as we shall see and anyway it is rather an unlikely option to be given to a prisoner of war. Many of the circumstances surrounding the manner in which prisoners of war were held in England at the time is told in the book *Prisoners of War in Britain*, and it is from this that we learn of the general conditions under which prisoners were held at the time of Lucien's arrival.[42] All prisoners of war came under the government department of the Royal Navy Transport Office, controlled by a Board of Officers headed by Admiral Sir Rupert George.[43] He became the first Controller to the Transport Board in 1809. Until then the system for holding prisoners had been developing on an *ad hoc* basis ever since the beginning of the Seven Years War in 1756 when prisoners began to arrive in significant numbers; seven thousand in the first year of the war which rose to forty thousand at the war's end in 1763. Most of those prisoners had been held in redundant warships or 'hulks' in appalling conditions, and some in temporary arrangements ashore. It was some thirty years before some substantial prisons were erected on land for holding prisoners of war. Approaching the turn of the century the prisoner of war population in Great Britain was again rising and reached 35,000 in 1798. Norman Cross, near Peterborough, was built to house 7,000 prisoners and Stapleton near Bristol was doubled in size to accommodate some 2,000.

By the time Lucien arrived there were some nine large prisons, including Dartmoor which had been built by 1809, in total housing some 40,000 prisoners. These arrangements were still inadequate and about fifty of the old hulks, anchored up in sheltered estuaries, were still in use and they had between them some 30,000 prisoners on board, who were kept in the same terrible conditions. Included in these figures were some officers who chose to stay with their men in either the prisons or the hulks as they were not prepared to swear an oath to remain on parole. Therefore they could make a legitimate attempt to escape and take up arms against England. However, the majority of officers were prepared to swear on their honour to behave as required by the parole conditions (ordinary seamen, and soldiers, apparently not considered to be 'gentlemen' and therefore to have no honour, were not given the choice). Most of these 2000 officers were divided up amongst the population of Great Britain in what were designated 'Parole Towns'. Naturally there were exceptions to the rule. Officers of General Rank were kept apart in other, usually more interesting, towns. Presumably the British hoped that this arrangement made it more difficult for senior officers to communicate with their men and start any form of prisoner insurrection.

Unsurprisingly, among the fifty parole towns listed in Great Britain, the greater number were at a distance from the sea, and of course therefore far from any chance of rescue by the 'Tyrant'. In the area around the Welsh Marches, and in particular Ludlow, the parole towns were quite concentrated: Abergavenny, Bishop's Castle, Bridgnorth, Montgomery, Newtown, Oswestry, Welshpool and Whitchurch. The reasons for such concentrations were not due to geographical circumstance alone but were to some extent dependent upon the personalities who occupied the positions of authority; and in this case Lord Powis.

Lord Powis or Edward Clive (1754-1839) 1st Earl of Powis (3rd Creation) was the son of 'Clive of India' and he, like his father, had already made a distinguished career in India and had been Governor of Madras. He had also been a Member of Parliament for Ludlow. He was very much a government man and someone the establishment would readily turn to in a time of trouble. Additionally he was very well placed to help as at this time Lord Powis was Lord Lieutenant of Shropshire and Montgomeryshire which meant that as well as being the personal representative of the monarch he also commanded the militia forces of both counties. It is not surprising therefore with ample militia at his command and the fact that he was already accommodating prisoners for the Transport Office at Lymore and in several county towns that it was not an unreasonable step of logic for the Government to ask Lord Powis, as a gentleman of 'rank', to see that Lucien and his party were settled in at Montgomery. In this case the Foreign Office rather than the Transport Office chose to continue to handle the matter of Lucien's imprisonment and all of the subsequent arrangements for his accommodation and his supervision. One final connection, and probably the most cogent, was that William Hamilton, the Permanent Under Secretary of State to the Foreign Office also happened to be the secretary for the Africa Association on whose committee Lord Powis sat. They would have known each other well and shared many interests. In this age of patronage most business, private and official, was conducted with people one knew and trusted or at the very least with those that had been introduced by a mutual friend. Hamilton therefore was able to provide his friend, Lord Powis, with an opportunity to serve both his country and his monarch. Naturally no reward or fee was ever given or sought; a nod of recognition from the King for services rendered was, of course, all the reward that one would desire.

Much of the individual detail in this narrative concerning this period which has not come from newspaper reports or the two Lucien *Memoirs* comes from archived material kept by the Foreign Office which is now in the National Archives at Kew. It is not a complete record and principally consists of letters and copies of letters, all written in manuscript, which were retained at the time and later bound together under a hardcover. There are many hundreds of the letters and in order not to clutter the narrative with individual references to each letter they are contained within the general references at note 44.

It was reported that Lucien and his suite landed in England at the Victualling Office quay at Plymouth on 20 December, having been brought to shore by the Admiral's cutter.[45] It is more probable that they landed as early as 18 December which was the date reported by Mr Mackenzie in a later letter. Lucien and his family were surprised and amazed at the 'immense concourse of spectators' that had gathered to see them come ashore. The family was met by a formal reception committee: Admiral Sir Robert Calder[46] who was Port Admiral Plymouth, General England[47], the Governor of Plymouth, Lord Boringdon[48] and several other naval and military officers. They were then taken in carriages, in procession, accompanied by the committee to the Kings Arms Hotel in Plymouth where it was planned that they would stay for several days and recover from the voyage.[49] This procession through the streets of Plymouth was seen by many including a Mr Redding who reported that he and his friends gave up their apartment in the Kings Arms to Lucien.[50] He described Lucien as 'a short, sallow man, not much like his illustrious brother, his family were with him - all Italian looking- his daughters, five in number, pretty, and two sons'.

Mr Colin Mackenzie, the individual named in the report above, was probably briefed verbally on his 'Commission' at the Foreign Office on the 19th as the letter instructing him is a file copy dated 21 December, by which time he had duly arrived at Plymouth. He travelled by 'express' coach and arrived, by twelve o'clock on Thursday 20 December, 'too late for Lucien Bonaparte who went out of town to return a visit from Lord Boringdon.'. Lucien had been quick off the mark to accept an invitation to Saltram, Lord Boringdon's home at Plympton.[51] Lucien may have been aware that it was a residence to rival many of the great and grand houses in Europe and home to a considerable art collection which included some ten portraits by Joshua Reynolds; even if he was unaware he would have been impressed and very appreciative of the chance to visit. Mr Mackenzie having read his instructions from the Foreign Office would have been less inclined to allow the visit, he wanted to get on as his instructions required:

> You will proceed without loss of time to Plymouth, for the purpose of communicating to Mr Lucien Bonaparte, his family, & suite, the nature of the arrangements intended for their reception and residence.

> You will inform Mr Lucien Bonaparte, that he is to proceed, for the present, together with his family and suite, to a country seat in the vicinity of the town of Ludlow which is ordered to be prepared for his temporary reception and residence.

> You will further inform him, that it is proposed that his permanent residence should ultimately be fixed at a seat at the Earl of Powis's, in the vicinity of the town of Montgomery, as soon as that place can be prepared for his reception.

> You will demand from him his <u>Parole</u>, for his family and suite, to be expressed in the form and terms of the annexed paper marked A, and to be given in the presence of Lieutenant General England – and you will acquaint him, if any objections should be offered on his part, that his parole is indispensably requisite.

> You will lose no time in arranging the removal of himself and the family from Plymouth.

> This will be done entirely at the expense of His Majesty's Government, unless it should appear that exorbitant claims are advanced by Mr Lucien Bonaparte, a compliance with which would be attended with unwarrantable expense.

You will not object, during the journey, to any proposal which may be made for halting, for a day or two, either at Barnstaple, or any other town upon the road.

For your expenses upon this service you will draw upon Mr Bidwell of this office, until you receive further instructions from me for the guidance of your conduct.

I am sir … [signed Wellesley]

Soon after his arrival Mr Mackenzie saw General England and informed him that Secretary of State, Lord Wellesley, wanted them both to witness the act 'when parole is taken', which they arranged to do the following day at 11 o'clock. Mackenzie then sat down, the afternoon of his arrival, to write his first letter to Mr William Hamilton, Permanent Under Secretary of State to the Foreign Office, in time to get the post to London.[52] He wrote that he understood that Lucien was 'in very good spirits but I fear not quite prepared for starting from this place as soon as I wish'. Mackenzie reported that people in Plymouth were more interested in 'invitations and visits' than moving Lucien on and that he has had difficulty in finding out just how many people Lucien had with him and just how much baggage; as he heard that it was 'very, very bulky'. He must have been under remit to describe Lucien but explained that he could not do so as he has not seen him yet and can report nothing 'except my having got thus far over the worst roads I have travelled in England'. He sounds like a man under pressure; 'I beg you will assure Lord Wellesley of my constant attention to fulfil his commission in every particular'. After signing off he adds an ominous post-script, 'I hear the Custom House officers have already found some articles marked as their prey'.

The weather was poor and the offloading of Lucien's baggage was delayed and consequently the Custom House could not check it. The delay was a huge frustration to Mackenzie. He was writing daily to Hamilton at the Foreign Office keeping him apprised of progress. He told them that as there was so much baggage most would have to remain in the warehouse. He also told them it was impossible to move the whole family at once and that Lucien understood the problems and was agreeable with his arrangements. Finally Mr Mackenzie had the satisfaction of reporting that he had obtained the article of parole duly signed. The parole document which was presumably translated into French by Mackenzie, is somewhat clumsy in style and translates into English as follows:

I declare, by this document, to have given my word of honour that neither I nor any of the members of my fam-ily or my retinue, named below, will stray beyond the boundaries which have been fixed or will be fixed by the

British Government during my stay in England, unless the permission has been given to me on behalf of
the said Government by the official authorities, and
moreover that I will not enter into any correspondence directly or indirectly with any enemy of His
British Majesty, will neither receive nor send any
letter or letters by any other means than the hands of
those that the said government names or will name to
this end in order for the letters to be read and
approved.

An image of the parole document is shown on the next page. It is signed
by Lucien Bonaparte, General England and Mr Mackenzie and lists both the
family members and the staff accompanying Lucien.

The family spent the next few days recovering at the King's Arms, which
included a family visit to the theatre to see Mr Philista's mechanical performan
ces.[53] The crowds followed them not only physically in Plymouth but also across
the country through the news reports. *The Ipswich Journal*, a town hundreds of
miles away on the east coast reported:[54]

The public anxiety at Plymouth, to see LUCIEN
BONAPARTE and his family, continues unabated. He
frequently comes to the windows, with his lady, to satisfy
the crowds that assemble in the street. A lady of the first
respectability in Plymouth attired herself in the dress of a
servant, at the Kings Arms, and carried in dinner, that
she might satisfy her curiosity with a view of the family.
The baggage of LUCIEN BONAPARTE and his attend-
ants, is stated to weigh 33 tons. There was a perfect
squabble among the inn-keepers of Plymouth and Dock,
to know which of them should have the honour of lodging these persons under his roof. Lucien studiously
avoids all pomp and ostentation. His eldest son, a fine
youth of 11 years of age [Charles-Lucien, in fact 7], was
on Tuesday taken through the dock-yard by Capt Warren
who brought them to England.

The newspapers incorrectly reported Lucien's departure, under the
arrangements of Mr Mackenzie, from Plymouth on Monday the 24th; they
actually left the day before on the Sunday. The same paper reported in the social
columns that the Earl of Powis had left his London house in Berkeley Square for
Shropshire. It was reported that Lucien 'having purchased a second hand travel-

ling chariot', had, according to another report, put an 'extraordinary' motto on it 'LUCEO NON URO' [I Shine Without Burning]. This is in all probability an example of journalistic licence as there is no other report of this decoration.[55]

Lucien was reportedly accompanied by his secretary. We might have assumed that this was M Servières, as he left Italy with Lucien, but he is not listed on the parole document and must have left Lucien's employment. The secretarial position was probably filled by M Châtillon. Travelling in the same carriage was his nephew, André Boyer, and two servants. With Mr Mackenzie in another chaise were his secretary and an interpreter. They must have started out rather late as they made only 33 miles before they stopped at the Clifford Arms, Chudleigh on the evening of the 23rd where they dined.[56] Mr Mackenzie found time to dash off a letter to Hamilton and tell him of their departure. *The Exeter Flying Post* reported them going through Exeter 'forenoon' on the 24th. They reached Street, in Somerset, that evening and spent the night of 24 December there 'at an excellent inn in an obscure situation.'[57] They would have left early next morning probably following the current route of the A39 road into Bath where fresh horses were waiting.

They were next reported as having stayed the night of Tuesday the 25th at the Kings Head at Gloucester, where Lucien 'walked out' for a while before supper (we should not be surprised that Christmas is not mentioned – that was a Victorian invention). Early the next morning he visited Gloucester Cathedral and soon after eight o'clock left for Tewkesbury. Here they had breakfast at the Hop Pole inn before heading for Worcester, where, without anyone alighting from the carriages, the horses were changed. Lucien was apparently pleased with the 'immense' crowd that assembled to see him but he did not delay and sped on to Ludlow. As the mileage from Gloucester to Ludlow is over sixty miles he was travelling fast and must have had to change horses often. It was reported that 'numerous groups of people were assembled in every town, village, and at every turnpike, through which they passed.' They could only have had a mere glimpse of the coach as it rushed by in a cloud of spray and mud. All things considered it was a very fast journey of some 250 miles and must have meant travelling for about 12 hours each day.

Madame Bonaparte and family were expected to follow on later in the week. With two wagon-loads of baggage they would have travelled at a considerably slower pace. Mr Mackenzie mentions none of this detail in his letter to Lord Wellesley on the 27th but informs him that the journey 'is completed', that they had arrived on Wednesday 26 December and that Lucien had already been introduced to the Earl of Powis and was appreciative of the attention he had received.

From an amalgamation of various reports it is clear that as Lucien approached Ludlow, Lymore had already been inspected by a J Bromfield Esq of Shrewsbury.[58] His estimate of the cost of repairs, or the time required to make them to the house, was such that the proposition of Lucien going there immediately was abandoned. We learn from Mackenzie that Lord Powis suggested that another of his seats, Stone House, five miles north of Ludlow at Onibury, might be suitable. Lord Powis, Lucien and Mr Mackenzie went there to inspect.[59] It was agreed by everyone that it was too small and although Lord Powis offered timber to have additional rooms built on it could not be made ready in time. Lord Powis then offered Dinham, his 'town house' in Ludlow, until the end of May. Lucien might have noticed it whilst walking around the ruins of Ludlow Castle earlier in the week, as it is close by the south wall, and hurried back to Ludlow for an inspection. Mackenzie also stated that Lucien intended to visit Lymore which he hoped would be ready by the summer.

The Hereford Journal, having made some comprehensive inquiries, brought the rest of the world up to date with the news that:

> LUCIEN BONAPARTE arrived at Ludlow about four
> o'clock on the evening of Wednesday [26 December]
> accompanied by his nephew, an interpreter, secretary, Mr
> Mackenzie, and a few servants. He drove to the Angel
> Inn, Broad Street, Ludlow where he dined and slept. On
> Thursday morning he walked about the town, viewed the
> Castle, and some of the principal streets; but as the
> weather was rather unfavourable and public curiosity
> great, he did not stay out long. On that evening one of
> the Winter Dancing Assemblies took place, which Lucien,
> his nephew, and some of his friends attended. Some of
> the latter danced, Lucien did not. He continued in the
> room until supper was announced; he then attended
> Countess Powis, and sat at her Ladyship's right hand
> during supper; after which he returned to the ball and
> card rooms. On Saturday [29 December], he went to The
> Stone House [sic], a seat of Lord Powis, about five miles
> from Ludlow, where Lucien is to reside in future, and
> from thence proceeded to Walcot, the principal residence
> of his Lordship, where he stayed a day or two, and
> returned to Ludlow.[60]

The newspapers stated that it was now generally expected that Lucien would remain for a week or ten days at Ludlow, the 'beauty of the environs appearing to attract his notice'. They said: 'Lucien was dressed in the English fashion, in a plain suit of black, a round hat, and hussar boots.' Ludlow citizens were told that Lucien's family had left Plymouth three days after him and were travelling with two wagon-loads of baggage by easy stages of 30 miles a day and were expected to arrive in a week. The press reported their progress at each stop. For instance at the stop to change horses at the Hop Pole in Worcester with the family in four carriages they reported 'Madame Lucien has a pleasing face, but seems to have suffered from fatigue: she is rather en bon point, and about 39 years of age; … A Physician and Abbé accompanied them, besides eleven domestic servants.'[61]

Lucien deemed Dinham suitable and arranged to move in immediately as he expected Alexandrine to arrive at any moment. He was just in time. *The Times* reports Madame Lucien and the four wagonloads of servants and baggage arriving at Ludlow on Wednesday 2 January. Mr Mackenzie reports the same and appears quite relieved and even excited by the event. His letter to Hamilton describes how the day unfolded:

> I learnt that Madame Lucien and her numerous family
> were approaching faster than we expected - M Boyer/the

nephew, and I immediately prepared to give them the meeting, with the agreeable information that Lucien had taken possession the evening before of Dinham House and that every requisite particular had been made for the whole party. We proceeded on the road only nine miles when we met the travellers who were delighted to think their journey so near an end and that the scramble of finding twenty beds at an Inn was not to be resumed. About two hours time brought us all to their quarters and I enjoyed the satisfaction of seeing the whole family meet again in high health, without encountering the smallest accident or interruption on the road – Madame L appeared highly pleased with the house which is larger than any that can be reasonably possessed in this quarter – she invited me to supper, and related with great spirit the different incidents which occurred from when we parted at Plymouth – the arrangements and directions we left on the road … the curiosity of the people which had exceeded any degree you can imagine, appears to have pleased the ladies, and the kindness and generous interest shown by all classes to assist them if anything could have been wanting appear to have made a strong impression. I find great pleasure in acquainting you that Lucien and his large party are now fixed to their satisfaction … [Lucien] has frequently assured me that he feels very much indebted to Lord Wellesley and expressed his gratitude to Lord Powis for the generous particulars offered him. I expect his Lordship here today and will be happy to introduce him to the rest of the family who form an interesting circle. I have already mentioned the leading subject of your letter to Lord Powis who agrees with me that ten miles around Ludlow would be quite sufficient.   As for the [narrative?] and assessment of Lucien and his family – I beg leave to submit it to Lord Wellesley, having ascertained that there is no town within that limit, nor any class of people who can interrupt him in his walks or rides; - the question of shooting occurred … Lord Powis has very kindly said one or two might occasionally accompany his keeper, but the season and hilly country around do not appear likely to tempt any of them.

The entourage settled into Dinham House and started to unpack. The family had been on the move for 22 weeks and they must have been exhausted. Lucien probably did not tell them that this accommodation was only temporary and that he would need to find somewhere else to stay before the end of May. That news could wait awhile. For now everyone needed some sleep.

Dinham House, Ludlow.

CHAPTER FOUR: THE DINHAM PRISON

For the first few days in Ludlow one might imagine that Lucien and his family remained within the house, catching up on sleep and sorting out both themselves and the children and trying to establish some sort of routine for the staff. The reverse seems to be the truth and Lucien and his family swiftly engaged with Ludlow society. Mr Mackenzie is able to report to Hamilton on 12 January that there is 'not the least shadow of a reason' to send a person from the Alien Office to supervise Lucien. He assures Hamilton 'the whole family in question appearing the most retired and inoffensive I ever met with. I am convinced Lucien wishes to be as soon forgotten as possible, and the discipline of all connected with him is as complete as could be desired. He has been anxious to assure me that every hint I gave him about the habit of our people, and the necessity of keeping his servants within doors as much as possible should not be lost. The excessive mode of living he commenced upon is already reduced, and as all his servants are arrived with his baggage the establishment at Dinham House is as completely tranquil as any of its size in England.' Mackenzie informs Hamilton that the local people can see quite an advantage in trading with the family as 'everything is paid for on delivery', nor has Lucien complained about the problems clearing his baggage at the Plymouth Custom house though Mackenzie reminds Hamilton that a 'great many cases' remain to be cleared. He also informs the Foreign Office that the House of Baring Brothers, which we now understand are Lucien's bankers in England, have informed him that the house and park at Hampton Court (at Dinmore, Herefordshire) is available for a 'moderate' rent (apparently £400 per annum – rather less than Lucien expected) and that Lucien wishes to have a look at the property.

One might make the assumption that in the late Georgian period the pace of life might be somewhat slower than it is now aided as it is by modern communications. Yet in a bare ten days Lucien has organised his household, established links with his bank, spent money quite lavishly and started house hunting as he knew that he had only a few months to make the arrangements. It is no surprise to find that he had also written several dozen letters to anyone he could think of who might be able to help him.

The Barings involvement with Lucien is instructive and demonstrates the reach of English banks at the time. The two generations of Barings before the this one already had a long history of financial dealings on the continent. They were probably involved in the transaction set up between the Portuguese and the Spanish Governments when Lucien was Ambassador to the Spanish Court. We recall that Lucien made a great deal of money for 'facilitating' this arrangement. Barings were obviously keen to continue to assist Lucien and had showed no moral objection in dealing with a person so closely associated with the enemy.

It is clear from comments in the almost daily letters to and from Hamilton that the Foreign Office was keen to hear, from Mackenzie, Lucien's reasons for splitting with Napoleon. As yet Mackenzie reports that he had not yet had the right moment to ask; they had travelled in separate carriages on the way to Ludlow and although he saw him daily since their arrival, Lucien was reticent to discuss the matter and Mackenzie felt he needed to wait for the right moment. It is also clear that Lucien is already networking and making contact with Barings not only to arrange his finances and sort out the letters of credit expected from Italy but also to help him find a suitable house. Furthermore, he has already raised the matter of the restrictions on his movement with Mackenzie and has asked whether he will be accorded the same privileges as some of the French Generals in England; Lucien is clearly aware that a General Lefèbreve at Cheltenham has been allowed to visit Bath for instance.

In any 'run-of-the-mill' appointment the agent selected by the Transport Board to administer prisoners would be appointed as parole agent for the town. He would be required to see that the average number of 40 officer prisoners lodged under his charge fulfilled all their parole obligations. He was instructed to carry out several duties: to muster them twice a week, to minister to their needs, to pay them their allowances (prisoners with the rank of captain and above received 10/6d per week – to pay for their board and lodging), to act as their financial agent, to hear and adjust their complaints, and in general to act as much as their guide and adviser as their custodian. Prisoners had to remain within a mile radius of their lodging unless they obtained particular permission and were even ordered to be indoors at their lodgings by five o'clock in winter and eight in summer. Prisoners were also expected to behave decently and with due regard to the laws of England, and in particular were not to attempt to correspond with anyone in France without submitting all letters to the agent. The agent may also have been responsible for other classes of prisoner, i.e. non commissioned officers, ratings, soldiers or captured civilians, that happened to be lodged in the town. This class of prisoner was not offered parole and would have been secured when not on work details. As they would have been under constant supervision by militia they were of less concern to the agent.

Lucien was of course treated as a special case. The principal difference being that it was the Foreign Office that had chosen to administer him and not the Transport Office. By 18 January the Foreign Office had enough information from Mr Mackenzie to draw up the set of rules by which they wished Lucien to live. It now becomes clear that Mackenzie is to be recalled and replaced by another as Hamilton sent instructions to Mackenzie to personally brief the man, not yet named, who was to take over from him:

> you should take an early opportunity of making known to Mr Lucien Bonaparte that he will conform himself to the following Regulations:
>
> That he shall consider the Town of Ludlow as the place of Residence for himself and family.
>
> That neither he, nor any person of his family or suite, exceed the limits of ten miles distance in their excursions out of Ludlow, without the express permission of one of His Majesty's Principal Secretaries of State.
>
> That he is to consider, from the date of your departure from Ludlow [Blank] as the person appointed by the government to superintend his conduct and that of his

family and to be the channel of communication between him and His Majesty's ministers.

I am further directed to acquaint you that it is the Marquess Wellesley's wish that upon your delivering over Mr Lucien Bonaparte into the charge of [Blank] you should give him, in writing, the substance of the written and verbal communications you have had from his Lordship, respecting the mode of treating Mr Lucien Bonaparte, in order that it may serve Mr [Blank] as a Rule of Conduct, as long as he continues in that employment. A copy of this minute you will have the goodness to enclose to me for Lord Wellesley's information.

I am further directed to acquaint you that Lord Wellesley will recommend the sum of £200 should be given to Mr [Blank] as an outfit and £500 per annum, as a compensation for his time in attending upon Mr Lucien Bonaparte, and to cover all personal expenses attending upon that charge, other than what extraordinary circumstances may render necessary: in which case it will be open to the discretion of His Majesty's Secretary of State to decide upon the form and extent of remuneration.

You will acquaint Mr [Blank] that it will be expected that he should transmit to this office a daily report of every circumstance of importance which may occur during his superintendence of Mr Lucien Bonaparte's family.

I am, sir, your most obedient, humble servant.

Most of what we learn about Lucien and his family's imprisonment comes from contemporary reports. His own *Memoirs* go into little detail and later biographies have chosen not to investigate this period. Perhaps it was a period the family wished to forget and yet like all experiences it could have had a profound effect on those who lived through it. Some of these effects will be addressed later on. In today's world of 'celebrity culture' this period and this event have some interesting parallels.

For citizens of Ludlow today it is instructive to see from the reports how the national interest in Lucien translated into the exposure of a small country town in the Welsh Marches. For some two hundred years Ludlow had attracted local country squires whose families wanted a taste of town life; to attend the theatre, balls and assemblies and the races. Ludlow already had a social reputation and even some 'celebrities' such as Lord Powis or R P Knight Esq. who would have already drawn some nationwide attention to Ludlow.[62] Admiral Nelson's visit in 1802 would also have been widely reported but in general terms there were not many inducements for the visitor from distant parts to take the trouble to come to Ludlow.

Ludlow from the east in 1810 by William Gwynn. Dinham House lies
midway between the church of St Laurence and Ludlow Castle.
Image courtesy of Ludlow Historical Research Group (LHRG).

'Tourists' or those who set out on tours of the country was a term that was just becoming to be known. For instance tours or visits to the River Wye through the Forest of Dean and Tintern Abbey had been promoted by the Reverend William Gilpin and people were starting to travel purely to see sights in England, as opposed to making pilgrimages, just as Englishmen had been doing on the continent for some time. Apart from having a ruined castle and being in a pleasant rural situation, Ludlow had little to attract visitors. Many travellers would make an overnight stop on their way to the spa towns of Wales but few would come to Ludlow for its own sake. Lucien's arrival was to change that for a short while and this can best be followed by selecting in a chronological order a variety of reports from across the country. It should be remembered that all local newspapers would be largely repeating the same words as those of the London papers. Thus what was reported in, for example, *The Aberdeen Journal* had probably been reported within the past week by *The Morning Chronicle* in London. The reports shown in the narrative have been chosen to illustrate the geographical breadth of the interest in Lucien and the events in Ludlow; they by no means show the complete extent of the coverage which would have been country wide.

Outside the walls of Dinham the excitement at the arrival of Lucien and his family in England had hardly abated. The reports of their progress were still doing the rounds of the provincial papers but it is very noticeable that most of these had started to caveat their reports by adding editorial comments that indicated that in their view the English nobility were paying rather too much attention to the arrival of this prisoner of war. The pendulum of public opinion, right across the country, had started to swing in a less self-congratulatory direction.

15 January 1811. *The Manchester Mercury* reports:

> LUCIEN BONAPARTE is a stranger, and may be received with civility; but it is really disgraceful to our national character, that people of rank should be seen truckling (sic) to the brother of the most treacherous and bloody tyrant that ever disgraced humanity; and so truckling too, for no other reason than because he his brother – the brother of the most rooted enemy of English freedom and happiness. Lucien has the means of procuring for himself all the comforts of life (how he obtained these means, it is not perhaps for us to enquire) but he certainly should be left to the spontaneous application of them in his own way; for he cannot be considered as deserving of that consideration and respect which have been shown to those illustrious foreigners who were obliged to seek an asylum in this country through the crimes and usurpations of his brother Napoleon.

14 January 1811. *The Hampshire Chronicle* chooses to report a quirky incident that occurred on Lucien's journey to Ludlow: 'At Exeter, Lucien was recognized by an invalid soldier, who had served abroad, and when the carriage stopped to change horses the soldier presented him with a paper, saying in French, that a lady in this country wished him to share in her smiles [presumably Lady Luck] as she had 44 capital prizes to bestow in the Grand State Lottery, the 15th next month, by a new order of drawing.' Perhaps the invalid soldier was selling lottery tickets and spotted an opportunity but one can hardly believe that

he recognized Lucien who had not been near a battlefield. We hear more of this incident a little later.

16 January 1811. *The Aberdeen Journal* presents the same sentiments using many of the same phrases as *The Manchester Mercury*. *The Northampton Mercury* on the 19 January does much the same but adds:

> We trust that our Princes and Nobles will not so much forget their own dignity and rank, as to associate familiarly with a foreigner, whose riches are not acquired by <u>honest</u> industry, or lawful inheritance, but whose notoriety in society originates chiefly from the very blameable share he had in a guilty brother's enormous preparations. Leave to our reformers the <u>honour</u> of fraternizing with this once <u>brother reformer</u>, but let all loyal Britons treat him with a generous and condescending, but distant civility.

This contrary opinion should not be overstated as throughout the country the 'public' cannot get enough detail of the family but already there are discernible differences of opinion in some quarters. An admittedly simplistic examination of those differences could be summed up as follows: the Tory faction, the monarchists and the government were deeply sceptical of Lucien's motives. The country had already given sanctuary to the Bourbons which was not universaly popular and there is a general fear of contagion by the revolution. Tories do not like the idea of Catholic emancipation and Lucien was Catholic, and yet the Pope had opened his ports to British ships and Lucien had the support of the Pope. There was of course 'noblesse oblige' but the principal benefit in securing Lucien as far as the Monarchy and the King's government are concerned is that they are much happier knowing that they now have Lucien in sight and under control. The opposition, the Whigs, who supported emancipation of the Catholics in England, were more prepared to accept Lucien at face value. Philosophers, writers, poets, and romantics would always be keen to hear and discuss fresh ideas and seek out the company of those who can write or who have made dramatic gestures such as having 'given up a kingdom for the love of a woman'. The greater majority though will sway with the tide of opinions as they are presented in the magazines and papers of the day. Those families who supplied the soldiers, sailors and marines to the maelstrom of war will have had a more personal view and would need to be persuaded to treat the enemy with anything other than extreme sanction. The militia and reservists would be excited to know that despite the threat of invasion apparently diminishing they still have their importance as guardians against any insurrection of prisoners and so keep their standing in the community.

In Ludlow, at this time, as in most places the prevailing opinion would be uncritical. Here is a man who has defied the TYRANT, HURRAH! What does he look like? What do they look like? What are they wearing? Everyone is doing their utmost to catch a glimpse of the family. Meanwhile those that cannot get to see these celebrated visitors have to put up with some conflicting reports: 'Madame Bonaparte is stout.' 'Madame Bonaparte is extremely handsome and fascinating; Lucien's daughter, of whom so much has been said, has great claims to a gentile figure, and elegant demeanour; but she is not beautiful.'

Means of communication and the passage of information between cities at this time were improving rapidly. As we have already understood from a newspaper report there was for instance a telegraph system in place for military use – albeit a visual semaphore system - from London to Plymouth when Lucien disembarked.[63] It was rudimentary but it worked when the weather did not interrupt it. The coach system was efficient and newspapers would have arrived daily at The Angel Hotel, Ludlow, and within 24 hours of being published. As the turnpike roads improved coaches could travel at speeds of up to 10 miles per hour and so in 1810 the 160 mile journey to London could be achieved with only one overnight stop.

As mail comes and goes by these coaches it is very possible to deal quickly with matters as they arise. In the last few days before Mr Mackenzie's departure Lucien wanted to clear up some outstanding issues. He asked for a letter to go to his bankers and Mackenzie duly sent it to the Foreign Office. He also raised the question of his impounded baggage and asked Mackenzie to plead to Lord Wellesley that as he is a prisoner of war he should not have to pay duty on his baggage. Mackenzie obliged and the letter was sent off with an enclosed list of the baggage concerned. The usual quick response was not forthcoming, and it was eight days before a reply was received. When we look at the items on the list, for example: '7 Cases assorted bottles [presumably wine], 1 case Kirsch, Rum etc., 1 case Tea, 1 case coffee, 3 demijohns of oil, 2 cases kitchen utensils … ', - it is clear that the Foreign Office would have been obliged to seek Treasury advice and that they in their turn would have contacted the Custom House. So perhaps we should consider that it was a quick response. The photograph on the next page is the first page of the list and gives a good indication of what Lucien considered important to take with one when emigrating to the unknown.

The Foreign Office answered in a fashion we would recognise today, that:

> it would not be possible, consistently with the
> uniform practice of the Treasury in cases which might be
> considered as having an analogy to the present, to permit
> the delivery of all the effects of Mr Lucien Bonaparte
> Duty Free: But that it does not appear that there would be

an objection to permitting such of those effects as Mr Lucien Bonaparte may not require for the use of himself and his suite to remain in the King's Warehouses without payment of Duty, until it shall be ascertained in what manner he would ultimately wish them to be disposed of … [and until that time the effects would remain where they were].

Note des Effets de Mr. Lucien Bonaparte.

7. Caisses de vins en bouteilles.
1. Caisse de Kirsch, Rhum &.
1. Caisse de Thé.
1. Caisse de Cire et de Caffé.
3. Damigeanes d'huile.
2. Caisses d'ustensiles d'office et de Cuisine.
7. Caisses de Pendules avec leurs cloches de Cristal.
1. Caisse de fraguements d'antiquités trouvées à Tusculum.
5. Caisses de bustes de marbre de Monsieur, Mad.e et des Enfants.
1. Caisse bibliotèque d'enfant.
9. Caisses de gravures des tableaux de Monsieur.
4. Ballots de tapis d'appartement.
9. Caisses de Porcelaines.
2. Caisses de verrerie et faïance.
2. Caisses de Sabres et fusils de Chasse.
2. Caisses de flambeaux dorés.
1. Caisse d'urvase d'albâtre.
5. Caisses de rideaux de mousseline et de soie en œuvre.
5. Caisses de glaces de diverses grandeur.
2. Caisses de deux bustes en marbre; du Pape.
2. Caisses de Guirguols et de flambeaux.

The first page of the list of Lucien's effects.

Lucien's reaction to this news can only be imagined as there was no letter recorded. He then tried another tack and wrote to Lord Wellesley and complained that he found the constraints put on him by the rules concerning his correspondence intolerable and implies that they are new, i.e. devised especially for him. Lord Wellesley directs, in a scribbled note on the letter, that 'Mr Mackenzie should appraise L B that the regulation is not new'. To add to his woes Lucien would have been well aware of the newspaper reports we have seen earlier, as would most people in Ludlow, particularly those concerning how he might have acquired his wealth. He may have felt the need to promote himself a little. Whether it was his natural instinct to assist the poor or whether it was a clear attempt at propaganda the following report indicates that Lucien had learned a thing or two about how to manipulate the newspapers to his own advantage.

23 January 1811. *The Hereford Journal* inserts a single sentence within a column: 'It is understood LUCIEN BONAPARTE has given £100 to be distributed to the poor of Ludlow.'

A letter dated 30 January is sent from Ludlow to Mr Hamilton in a new hand informing him that 'everything here with respect to Mr Lucien Bonaparte and his family has gone on satisfactorily.' The letter is signed by Mr William Dickinson who we can now assume has succeeded to the post which Mr Colin Mackenzie had formerly occupied.[64]

2 February 1811. *The Morning Post* reports: 'The reason assigned to Lucien's desire to visit London is that having purchased several tickets in the present state lottery he is anxious to see the new method of drawing the 44 capitals in one day - how the £200,000 prizes will be distributed on Friday 15 February.' This report must have been related to the earlier story from Exeter. In any event it might have provided a plausible excuse to visit London. Lucien was keen to get to the centre of things, to the seat of government – no doubt to press for his release. It should be understood that the government is less keen to see him. The French King, Louis XVIII has lived in England since 1808. He and his enormous retinue of courtiers, some 100 of them, were living at Hartwell House, just outside Aylesbury, Buckinghamshire. Others of the Bourbon King's French court, such as the Comte D' Artois, were living in London. All of them were very much under the protection of the Prince of Wales – who was acting as Regent due to the illness of his father George III, and neither he nor the French King were likely to have wanted Lucien anywhere near them and as far as we know the visit never took place.

2 February 1811. *The Ipswich Journal* stated:

Several strangers visit Ludlow daily to see LUCIEN BONAPARTE and the family, and they, knowing the public curiosity, generally walk for an hour or two round the castle. One day due to bad weather they did not and a man who had come a distance was so disappointed he sent his compliments and begged a viewing for a few seconds, Lucien desired the stranger to be shown in, made him sit down and gave him two or three glasses of excellent wine.

3 February 1811. The *Bury and Norwich Post*: 'LUCIEN BONAPARTE now walks the streets of Ludlow without the least annoyance from popular curiosity. He lives very retired, and devotes several hours in the day to reading.'

We know that almost immediately after Lucien's arrival he knew that he could not remain at Dinham. He needed a larger house but Ludlow could not provide it. In any case, pleasant as he said he found Ludlow, being a public spectacle was proving annoying. He was clearly not going to have the freedom of movement he wanted within England. He decided that he would rather try and seek permission to continue his journey to America. According to one report Lucien wrote directly to the Prince of Wales.[65] He could not have sought a higher authority and he probably thought that by circumventing the bureaucrats he had a better hope of a positive response. As he waited for the reply the papers continued to give their readership some more detail of the prisoner and his family.

27 February 1811. *The Hereford Journal wrote*:

LUCIEN BONAPARTE, in his comfortable retreat at Ludlow, has composed an epic poem, of considerable length, which he entitles *Charlemagne* intending it for speedy publication. The few who have seen it, speak highly of the poetic beauties with which several of its episodes abound. The property brought over by this brother of the Tyrant amounts to £100,000 in good bills duly honoured by British merchants. With the interest thence arising, he contrives, by economical arrangement, to keep an elegant table, and an establishment of 30 domestics. He takes great delight in the education of his eldest daughter, a beautiful and accomplished girl, about 15 years of age, and proposes, if the government indulges him by a continued residence in this country, which he so much admires, to devote a portion of his time to the practice of English Agriculture, which he is greatly pleased with.

At this point Mr Dickinson's appointment as Lucien's 'commissary' came to a swift end and it is clear that Lord Powis was asked to recommend another. Lord Powis chose Lieutenant Colonel Leighton, a retired army officer, who lived in Shrewsbury and was currently commanding the Shrewsbury Volunteers.[66] Lord Powis in his role as Lord Lieutenant would have been his direct superior and would have known him well.

There can be little doubt that the principal cause for Dickinson's removal was the letter he 'permitted' Lucien to send to the Prince Regent. The Lucien *Memoirs* suggest that he was removed for showing 'too much indulgence towards his prisoners'. He may well have done so. In addition to poor control of the prisoner's letters Dickinson may also have permitted, or at least not prevented his prisoner from roaming beyond his bounds. A report, some years later in *The Hereford Journal*, stated that 'A gentleman visited Shakespeare's house at Stratford and copied from the walls the lines written there by a celebrated foreigner:[67]

> The eye of genius glistens to admire
> How memory hails the sound of Shakespeare's lyre;
> One tear I shed, to form a crystal shrine,
> To all that's grand, immortal, and sublime! '
> March 4, 1811   LUCIEN BONAPARTE.

The Foreign Office letter appointing Colonel Francis Leighton was dated 1 March 1811 and directs:

> that upon the recommendation of the Earl of Powis, it has been judged expedient to appoint you for the present to the charge of superintending the person and family of Mr Lucien Bonaparte during his residence in England.
>
> Mr Dickinson the person now residing at Ludlow in that character will be desired to introduce you to Mr L Bonaparte and to put you in possession of any information which he may judge useful to promote the good of the service in which you are employed.
>
> The Marquess Wellesley desires that you should take an early opportunity of making known to Mr Lucien Bonaparte that the British Government will expect, during his residence in England, or until the further pleasure of His Majesty's Government shall be expressed to

him through the proper channels, that he will conform himself to the following regulations:

1. That he shall consider the town of Ludlow, or any place within two miles distance of that town as the place of residence for himself and family.

2. That neither he nor any person of his family or suite shall exceed the limits of ten miles distance in their excursions outside of Ludlow without the express permission of one of His Majesty's Principal Secretaries of State.

3. That from the date of your introduction to him he is to consider you as the person appointed by the Government to superintend his conduct, and that of his family and to be the channel of communication between him and His Majesty's Ministers.

I am further directed to acquaint you that it is the Marquess Wellesley's wish that upon your arrival at Ludlow you should obtain what information may be in your power with respect to the most eligible mode of ensuring Mr Lucien Bonaparte's compliance with that part of his parole by which his correspondence is restricted.

I am further directed to acquaint you that Lord Wellesley will recommend that the sum of £200 shall be given to you as an outfit, and that the sum of £500 shall be paid to you annually from the 25th day of February 1811 in compensation for your time in attending upon Mr Lucien Bonaparte , and to cover all personal expenses attending upon that charge, other than what extraordinary circumstances may under necessary: in which case it will be open to the discretion of His Majesty's Secretary of State to decide upon the form and extent of remuneration.

The Marquess of Wellesley desires that you will transmit to this office a daily report of every circumstance of importance which may occur during your superintendence of Mr Lucien Bonaparte and his family. – For this purpose it will be necessary that you should take up residence in the town of Ludlow, and that you should be

> present with Mr L Bonaparte or his family, at least once
> every day.'

The Foreign Office was already aware that Lucien was using the services of Baring Brothers. We can assume that they had instructed the bank that they wished to see all of Lucien's correspondence as Alexander Baring, a partner, reluctantly informs them by letter, 12 March 1811, from Portman Square, 'I have little doubt that the enclosed is very innocent … '[68] Having facilitated the sale to America of Louisiana by the French in 1803 thereby enabling Napoleon to fund his war one could expect that the Foreign Office was not necessarily inclined to take this bank's opinion entirely at face value and wished to make their own judgement as to what was to be considered innocent.

His Majesty's Treasury had by this time heard that the Custom House had completed the examination of the effects that Lucien had left in Plymouth. They informed the Foreign Office, who in turn informed Lucien of those items that could be delivered to him free of duty. As one might expect the list did not include the 7 cases of wine, or the Kirsch, or the tea or the coffee. The three cases of 'Porcelaine' and two of 'verrerie et faÿance' were also retained along with several others cases. The common factor amongst those items held was perhaps that they could be considered goods that might be sold for profit. Lucien would not have been a happy man.

13 March 1811. *The Hereford Journal* started another rumour by stating with absolute certainty:

> LUCIEN BONAPARTE is removing from Dinham house
> to Ludford house, the seat of Mr Charlton, whose
> mansion is more capacious than his present residence,
> more contiguous to Ludlow, and environed by a domain
> which excludes him from the numerous intrusive visits
> he has been exposed to at Dinham House.

Mr Dickinson's letter to Hamilton four days later makes it clear that he considered that he had now handed over his duties to Colonel Leighton. Leighton wrote to Hamilton that he met with Lucien on the 13th and informed him of the conditions set out by the Foreign Office. He then explained in a lengthy letter that Lucien 'expressed much surprise & discontent' at being limited to two miles from Ludlow in which to seek a residence as it was an impossibility to find a house large enough for his family. Leighton went on to say that Lucien 'expressed his dissatisfaction in as strong terms as he could consistently with respect'. Leighton said that he had apprised Lord Powis of the conversation and that he had learned that Lucien was contemplating moving to a house near Ross in Herefordshire.

Colonel Leighton then asked for a copy of the parole document as he had not been able to obtain a list of the people accompanying Lucien. It was also apparent that the speed with which he had been required to take up his post had not permitted him to sort out his own affairs and he informed Hamilton that he would be using Dickinson's accommodation for the time being. By 6 April Leighton had not seen any sign of the salary, or the 'outfit', promised to him and he asked Hamilton how he was to draw it.

Colonel Leighton settled to his task quickly and wrote almost every other day to Hamilton. He informed him that he had made an arrangement with the post mistress in Ludlow that unless she saw his 'secret' mark on the letters from Lucien or his family she was to retain them for his inspection. In this way he hoped to stop any clandestine correspondence. He also added that he had been making some local enquiries:

> The most intimate acquaintance which Mr Lucien Bonaparte has in Ludlow is a Mr Lowe, of whom I can learn nothing to excite suspicion. He was here some time before the former arrived in England; & I find upon enquiry that his correspondence, tho tolerably large, has not increased since the period, to which my enquiries naturally tended. He is a Scotch-man [sic], & a man of letters, to which latter circumstance the intimacy is generally attributed by the inhabitants of this place.

The difficulties encountered over the superintendence of the mail to and from Lucien and his retinue was a subject that caused endless concern to all parties. Lucien, with the help of his secretary, quite often produced several letters per day. No matter where he finds himself Lucien uses letters to implore, plead and persuade others to do his bidding. We have already seen his readiness to try and influence events from his ship in Cagliari and his prison in Malta. His arrival in England brings no change in his behaviour and the letters continue to stream out – always in French. It was clear that Mr Dickinson's arrangements had not been good enough and he had had little control over Lucien's mail distribution. Lucien in turn had little faith in the ability of the Foreign Office to transfer his mail, once read, either onwards or to him. Lucien told Leighton that he was anxious to get hold of letters he believed had been sent to General Oakes, in Malta, from his servants in Tunis. He had allowed several of his staff to return to France via Tunis and wanted to know of their progress; as we deduced earlier from the absence of Servières name on the parole document this party must have included his former secretary and his family.

We should recall that Lucien has also been waiting for a reply from the Prince of Wales. We are informed, by a Dr Samuel Butler who we shall meet later, that Lucien had to wait six weeks for his letter to be returned unopened and with an 'intimation' that he must never presume in future to write direct to the Prince. This was in fact so and it fell to Colonel Leighton to return the letter into the hands of Lucien and inform him that 'any proposal or communication he wishes to make to HRH must be conveyed through the formal channel of the Prince's Secretary of State.' Butler also tells us that the 'fired' Lucien wrote to Lord Wellesley, Secretary of State for Foreign Affairs, stating that he was accustomed to writing direct to the Pope and several sovereigns of Europe, and believed that he should be exempt from official rules. However, and one can imagine the Gallic shrug, he agreed he would in future conform to the general custom.

After the rebuff concerning his letter to the Prince of Wales Lucien assumed that he was not going to be allowed to go to America and would have to remain in England. This realization provided the catalyst for a move to a bigger house and one that was as far removed as possible from the prying eyes of the public. Colonel Leighton, who may not have been aware of the perceived need to leave Dinham in May, reported to Hamilton that Dinham was not proving large enough to accommodate the family and servants. Mr Hamilton in response added a 'private' note (see below) to the letter to help lighten Leighton's burden a little: 'you need not absolutely confine him to 20 miles around – but avoid if you can going within ten miles of Shrewsbury.'

Armed with this information both Leighton and Lucien together, and sometimes independently of each other, put all their efforts into finding another residence. It would seem that that most of the large houses within 20-30 miles of Ludlow were considered.

One of the houses was Downton Hall, the home of the Rouse-Boughtons. This house lay some three miles to the north of Ludlow set in extensive parkland looking south to Titterstone Clee. We see in a copy of the letter Sir Charles Rouse-Boughton wrote to his son William, 11 April 1811, that he has had several meetings with Lucien in Ludlow 'who has repeatedly teased & importuned me to let him have Downton which I have finally declined for various reasons. Lord Powis has made himself unpopular by bringing him into that country [sic].'[69]

The search continued. Another house considered is an unnamed dwelling at Presteigne and Hamilton in a letter of 13 April gives his sanction for the move there. He also adds the news that the 'payment of passage' for those servants in Tunis will be effected by order of the Governor at Malta. No doubt Lucien was delighted to learn of this generosity but a cynic might say that it was General Oakes who wished to ensure that this encounter with the French was well and truly ended and that this payment was a convenient method of ensuring it.

Several sources cite anecdotes that some of the citizens of Ludlow had abused the family and had even attacked them and thrown stones at the house. The *Memoirs* do not mention this nor are there any reports in the paper; however, there does appear to be some truth to the reports. The facts reported by Leighton are that an 'unpleasant difference' between two inhabitants of Ludlow and two of Lucien's servants – 'circumstances too trifling' to mention have led to a 'bill of indictment for an assault' and that in due course the servants will have to appear at the assize (Ludlow Quarter Sessions). Leighton also reports that some of the Bonaparte family had complained that stones were thrown at them and their children both in their garden and in a public walk adjoining their house. Leighton informs Hamilton that he has 'hired a person to patrol in the hopes that the delinquents will be apprehended and punished'. He also enquires 'in what way is this expense to be defrayed? It will not continue long', he suggested as Lucien had made arrangements to take a house at Ashford, the seat of Mr Ricketts. This is Ashford Hall, a house built about 1760 and extended in the period 1771-74. It lies two miles south of Ludlow and is described in *A Description of the Town of Ludlow ...* 1812, 'as a neat mansion belonging to the family of the late G C Ricketts Esq. It stands on a moderate eminence a quarter of a mile from the banks of the Teme. An excellent garden, elegant plantations, rich sylvan scenery, verdant fields, and extensive views of the circumjacent [sic] country completes a scene of the most lively picturesque beauty.' The house had been occupied for nine years by George Crawford Ricketts before his death in 1811.

The *Memoirs* suggest that not only had Lucien 'courted with avidity' the principal inhabitants of Ludlow but that he freely entered into their parties and could claim that he had acquired 'their affection and esteem.' It is quite clear that Lucien and his family were sought after as guests by many of the estate owners and wealthy families around Ludlow. Lucien and Alexandrine would have been only too happy to get their family away from the relative confinement of the house and garden at Dinham and the stares of the townsfolk and into an environment where they could relax and share the pleasures of music, singing and acting. Even to talk in a mutually familiar language such as French would have been a relief. Lucien would have been keen to discuss world affairs with educated men, view collections of paintings and converse on matters of the arts and nature. There were several such families around Ludlow most of whom would have had some member of the family who had made an excursion onto the continent of Europe on 'tour'. There were indeed some who had an intimate knowledge of Rome and a profound knowledge of the classics which would have been of particular interest to Lucien as he tried to complete his 'poem', *Charlemagne*. This sort of association with other men of letters and their families must have had some influence on both Lucien and his family. Admittedly this is speculation but nevertheless deserves to be explored particularly as other accounts largely underrated or even ignored their time in England.

No literary references have come to light to prove a connection between Lucien and one of the foremost and intellectually distinguished families around Ludlow, that of the Knights at Downton Castle. There have been several anecdotal mentions of which the most plausible is that of Pauline Beesly in her paper, *A Brief History of the Knight Family* which states quite categorically that Lucien was entertained at Downton. It is hard to believe that Lucien would not have visited this castle lying as it does just six miles from Ludlow. Its position overlooking the river Teme is in a very private but universally recognized 'picturesque' landscape. It had the additional attraction of a history of ironworking, which was of interest to Lucien, as well as being the site of horticultural experimentation. There was space for children to roam on foot or horseback and thus on the face of it Downton offered the potential for the enjoyment of the whole family.

The builder and owner of Downton Castle, Richard Payne Knight, now 61, was a renowned connoisseur and collector. Payne Knight had also been a Member of Parliament but more pertinently was a scholar who had published several books including his didactic poem *The Landscape*, in 1794. A more recent publication, *The Progress of Civil Society*, would have given them rather more to talk about as it dealt, in part, with the French Revolution. They perhaps could even have talked of the benefits of moving to America, which Payne Knight had

considered when he was being vilified by the press. As a member of the prestig-
ious Society of Dilettanti he had friendship or acquaintance with most of
cultured society in England. Payne Knight had a respectable collection of paintings and a very special collection of Claude Lorrain drawings of Rome as well as
several Etruscan artefacts purchased from his friend Sir William Hamilton,
Ambassador to the King of Naples, some of which may have come from the area
of Tusculum and Lucien's own estate at Frascati.

Undoubtedly Lucien and his family would have appreciated the Ludlow
countryside. The rolling hills and fields of Canino in the Italian spring enjoying
much of the same lush growth as Herefordshire and Shropshire. They would
have been even more delighted to discover the similarities of their castle on the
Canino estate at Ponte del la Badia with Downton and of the river flowing
through a delightful gorge just as they found the River Teme did at Downton
(photo and illustration page 85).

At this time Payne Knight's brother, Thomas Andrew Knight, was resident
at the castle, Payne Knight preferring to spend more of his time at his house in
London. Thomas Andrew was a leading member of local society and nationally
recognized as a noted naturalist. It may well have been that it was Thomas
Andrew who entertained Lucien and from this meeting stemmed Lucien's
reported interest in English agriculture. [70]

For the past fifteen years Thomas Andrew Knight had been writing papers
for both the Royal Society and the Horticultural Society explaining his experi-
ments with plants, trees and animals. He was therefore friends with internation-
ally regarded men of science such as Sir Joseph Banks and Sir Humphry Davy.
In the first week after Lucien's arrival at Ludlow Thomas Andrew had been
elected President of the Horticultural Society, an appointment widely reported in
the press and of which Lucien would certainly have been aware.

As he was a relatively shy man it was most probably Thomas Andrew's
wife, Frances, a woman who loved entertaining, who would have invited the
family to Downton. Two of her daughters, Fanny (17) and Elizabeth (13) were of
similar ages to Alexandrine's girls and had the same well developed social skills.
It is for consideration that even the young Charles-Lucien, then aged eight,
would have had his imagination and enthusiasm fired by all the evidence of
naturalistic experimentation he would have found at Downton. He went on to
become a leading ornithologist, particularly of American birds and wrote several
books on zoology. One could easily imagine that Lucien and his family may
well have found new friends around Ludlow had he been able to stay.

Various theories have been advanced to explain Lucien's departure from
Ludlow. It is related that Lord Powis, an enthusiastic friend of Lucien at first,

was now cooling in his interest, even to the point that 'it was heard' that he wanted to charge Lucien rent. According to the *Memoirs* Lucien immediately offered 300 guineas to Lord Powis in payment, which was at first refused but, 'at length [he] consented to receive'. If there had been a misunderstanding and that report was true it is not difficult to conceive that, as the *Memoirs* state, Lucien felt 'obliged to quit Ludlow', but it seems more probable that practicalities and expediency, which had been known from first arrival, combined with a desire for less exposure to the public, drove the decision to move away from Ludlow.

17 April 1811. *The Morning Chronicle* and then *The Times*, on the following day, would appear to have been given the 'official news release' and reported that; 'LUCIEN BONAPARTE, with his family, and servants are removing from the vicinity of Ludlow into Worcestershire.'

20 April 1811. Both *The Oxford Journal* and *The Sussex Advertiser* wrote or rather repeated a vitriolic report that it attributed to a Staffordshire newspaper:

> LUCIEN BONAPARTE, with his family, and his thirty Corsicans servants, are removing from the vicinity of Ludlow, into Worcestershire. Report in the neighbour-hood states this ex-prince and his crew to be purely French, as far as filth and decency can render them such. He has materially damaged the mansion he has resided in, it is said, by the style in which they have pigged together. His thirty servants, instead of lying in beds, were swung in hammocks from the ceilings, and eat together like so many wild Arabs. They are represented to be, altogether, a strange mélange of parade, of finery, and of filth! – (Stafford Paper).

At the same time others in the literary world made known their opinion of Lucien as we see from this letter of 21 April 1811, when Robert Southey wrote to Grosvenor C Bedford [71]:

> I have another piece of news, which did surprise me. Brougham has been commissioned to apply to my uncle for the purpose of discovering whether I would under-take to translate Lucien Bonaparte's poem. My uncle replied, he supposed not, but referred the plenipotentiary to me; and no further proceedings have taken place. When I hear from B, I shall recommend Elton for the task, who translates well, and will, probably, be glad of a task which is likely to be so well paid. This has amused me very much; but it has rather lowered Lucien in my

opinion, by the vanity which it implies. If his poem be good for anything, he may be sure it will find translators: it looks ill to be so impatient for fame as to look about for one, and pay him for his work. From whom the application to my worship came I do not know; Lucien has probably applied to some friend to recommend him to the best hand; and, dispatch being one thing required, the preference has, perhaps, on this score, been given to me over Mr. Thomas Campbell; by which, no doubt, I am greatly flattered.

A little later the letter below was sent to Mr Arkwright, of Hampton Court, Herefordshire.[72] This was the son of Sir Richard Arkwright, one of the first industrialists to devise a disciplined and profitable factory system in the cotton industry, who had bought Hampton Court in 1809. The letter demonstrates the wide extent to which Lucien and Leighton were casting their net to secure accommodation. The letter is from the Reverend Nicholas Waite Robinson, vicar of Bodenham, Herefordshire.

Ludlow 24 April 1811

Dear Sir,

As we are here upon a visit to Col Eyton.[73] I have had the pleasure of meeting with a friend of the name of Col Leighton who has the care of Buonaparte & knowing that we are living so near Hampton Court he appears anxious that I should write to you on the subject of letting Buonaparte that place, which I hope will be a sufficient apology for my troubling you with this letter. Buonaparte and his family wish to live in a retired a way as possible, he is now in treaty for Morley [sic] Sir Walter Blunt's House [sic], and has the refusal of it & it is certainly a delightful house but entirely without furniture. Mr Lechmere Charlton has made him an offer of Ludford which joins upon Ludlow, the rent was to have been £500 a year for a completely furnished house, a Park with 40 head of deer, 15 acres of land, a gardener & gamekeeper paid for by a Mr Charlton, this they have declined as Buonaparte can't bear living in or near a Town. Mr Nuttall [Arkwright's agent] I understand has written to you, & I shall be much obliged to you to write a line addressed to Lieut Col Leighton, Ludlow, as soon as it is convenient, as all negotiations between Col

Leighton &c for a house will be suspended till your determination respecting Hampton Court is known – should you have any fears about your furniture they would either purchase any part of it that is there, or buy the furniture they may want. Col Leighton thinks well of the conduct of Buonaparte since he has been under his care, & who I was told was hurt at your former refusal of Hampton Court to him, when your advertisement for letting it appeared in the very first Hereford Papers. Please excuse the haste in which I have written this letter as Col Eyton is waiting for me to go into the fields with his local Militia, which are by far the best disciplined of any I have seen, we have concerts & Balls every night & I shall enjoy our vicarage the more afterwards.   Mrs Robinson desires her respects to Mrs Arkwright &c.

& believe me, dear sir, yours most sincerely,
N W Robinson

1 May 1811. Colonel Leighton would appear to have been busy, taking just over a week to get his public relations system working and rebut the 'pigging' slander being heaped upon Lucien in the 'Staffordshire' paper. *The Hereford Journal* reported: 'We understand the account of LUCIEN BONAPARTE being about to leave Ludlow and reside in Worcestershire, is not correct. The illiberal paragraphs which have appeared in several papers concerning his family and servants are also untrue; the whole of the servants are Italians, and not Corsicans, and the conduct of Lucien since he has resided at Ludlow, has been highly correct, and all his pecuniary transactions marked by liberal and just punctuality.'

At this point news from Alexander Baring, the banker, of negotiations for yet another house, was related to Hamilton by Colonel Leighton in a letter dated 10 May. The letter tells us that the negotiations with regard to Mr Ricketts and his house, Ashford Hall, were failing and provides confirmation that Lucien was now discussing the possibility of going to Mawley Hall, near Cleobury Mortimer. Leighton obviously knew nothing of this change of plan and it indicated that Lucien was using some of his own contacts in his quest for a house. In this case it was probably the local Roman Catholic community who was helping, Mawley Hall being owned by Sir Edward Blount, a prominent and well established Roman Catholic in the area.[74]

A new problem arose the following week at one of Leighton's visits to Dinham. He was told by the family physician, Monsieur de France, that Madame Lucien had the beginning of a serious complaint and that it was necessary to have recourse to the Bath 'waters'. It was suggested that Abbé Charpentier would need to accompany her as he spoke some English. The following day Leighton reported that Lucien now wished to go as well, and to take his whole family, apparently citing that other military prisoners of war had been permitted to visit Bath and that failure to allow this visit may 'excite an anxiety of mind' in his wife. It would seem highly likely that this was an attempt by Lucien to push his boundaries and see if he can get Colonel Leighton and the Foreign Office to accommodate him. Leighton forwarded this request but there is no record of either a visit to Bath or an acknowledgement that he was awaiting permission to go there. The matter seems to have been shelved.

22 May 1811. *The Hereford Journal* reported that 'LUCIEN BONAPARTE lost a sum of some £8000 in a London bank failure having remitted the sum from Malta.' According to the *Memoirs* the bank was owned by a Le Mesurier, a French born banker.[75] A little research informs us that a company called P & H Le Mesurier & Co did in fact suspend business in 1811 and it would seem that this bank was the likely culprit.[76]

Colonel Leighton's report of 23 May 1811 showed the exasperation he felt at Lucien's house hunting efforts as he stated 'it will be a long while before he fixes his residence'. His next report however, was more cheerful and included the news that Lucien had found a house near Worcester. Leighton positively assured Hamilton that the location should not be a problem and added that the house belongs to a Mr La Motte (sic) and is called Thorngrove. No doubt Leighton felt he could relax a little and start to look to his own affairs as he added to his report that he had asked Mr Thomas Eyton to 'receive what may be due to me on account of this service'. This initiative to get a friend, who was going to London, to call in at the Foreign Office and get a bankers draft indicated that Colonel Leighton has had enough of waiting for 'government' to pay him. It was not in fact until 22 June that the patient Colonel wrote to acknowledge that he had received £380 11s for his services, including the 'outfit', since he took over the task in early March.

Later that week, on the Friday, Leighton wrote, 'I am going this day with M Boyer and Lucien Bonaparte to Worcester to make arrangements for Lucien Bonaparte to see the house tomorrow. He has been told he could be in possession in a month.' All was going well. On 2 June Leighton informed Hamilton that Lucien was now to get the House of Baring to 'treat' on his behalf. The only objection Leighton can see 'is the tenure by which it is held, it being lease hold from the Bishops of Worcester'. He believed that this matter would soon be cleared up. He hoped that Hamilton would have no objection to him, (Leighton) 'being stationed' in Worcester.

There are indications that Lucien's first offers for Thorngrove were not accepted. No letters have come to light except the sudden announcement from Leighton that 'it will surprise you Lucien Bonaparte has decided to take Morville Hall, the seat of Mr Hanbury-Tracey'. Morville Hall is close to Bridgnorth, Shropshire.[77] So all change. But no! Two days later Leighton wrote again 'I have to inform you that Mr La Motte has accepted Lucien Bonaparte's offer'. So the Thorngrove initiative was back on track once again.

An interesting note in an article in a publication called *Hoggs Weekly Instructor* some years later explained how Lucien managed to buy a property in England.[78] The article was entitled *British Laws affecting Aliens* and states:

> as the law stood prior to 1844, aliens in great Britain were debarred from the possession of real property … [Each alien, however] was permitted to hold thousands of pounds in funds. In some instances the laws were evaded by [property] being held in trust for foreigners; and Lord Ashburton stated, in his evidence before a select committee of the House of Commons on these laws, that he had held an estate in Worcestershire for LUCIEN BONAPARTE. His Lordship said – "Mr Perceval was then Prime Minister: I asked him if he had any objection, and he said ' You are, of course, aware that the crown may seize it at any time' I stated that to LUCIEN BONAPARTE, and he said he was willing to take it upon those terms, if there was no objection to it being so held, and I held it for a time."

Lord Ashburton (1774-1848) was simply Alexander Baring at the time, an MP, and as we already know, a partner in Baring Brothers & Co. It was not until 1835 that he became 1st Baron Ashburton, following his tenure as Master of the Mint from 1834 to 1835. There are indications that Barings warned Lucien of the impending failure of the French bank mentioned earlier which allowed him to retrieve some of his funds before the final collapse.[79]

The purchase of Thorngrove from Mr John Lagier Lamotte, a domiciled Frenchman, was enabled by Barings on Lucien's behalf.[80] The *Memoirs* stated that the sum of £9,000 was paid for the estate. Alexander Baring informed the Foreign Office by letter that £13,500 was the sum (perhaps £734,000 in 2012).[81]

Most accounts now tell us that at around this time Lucien tried to raise some money. It was not surprising given his recent expenses and losses at the bank. Nor was he living frugally, that had never been his style, even when he was borrowing money heavily. There are indications that he felt he needed to live in a manner appropriate to his 'rank' and was willing to spend accordingly. Some of his servants wore liveried uniform and there are several references to the extensive and sumptuous meals he provided for visitors. He wrote to his fellow brother-in-exile, Louis, ex-King of Holland, asking for money, which seemed to be promised but never actually materialized.

The next newspaper report dated 19 June 1811 may have been related to these money raising activities. *The Bury and Norwich Post* reported: 'The immense pier[82], Paris plate, glasses, and Brussels carpet, the property of LUCIEN BONAPARTE, were sold by public auction at Plymouth on Friday, at a very high rate'. This presumably was some of the remaining baggage unloaded from the *President* that had been kept in store and was awaiting payment of duty before transport to Ludlow. We see from the next report that the house at Thorngrove came complete with furniture and he may well have decided that he could dispense with the surplus personal effects he had brought and raise some cash. He clearly did not sell everything. Later reports have indicated that Lucien received at Thorngrove sufficient of his paintings and collected artworks to set up a small museum.[83] We know from the early lists that his baggage had indeed included a crate of artefacts from Tusculum.

3 July 1811. *The Hereford Journal* reported: 'Thorngrove House, near Worcester, the seat of J Lamotte Esq., has been recently purchased with the furniture, for LUCIEN BONAPARTE, who removed there from Ludlow on Monday last.' The dates given for Lucien's actual arrival at Thorngrove are confusing, no doubt arising from elements of the family either getting there earlier or remaining longer than others at Dinham. T C Turberville in his book, *Worcestershire in the Nineteenth Century*, published in 1852 gives the date as 31 May 1811. Thomas Wright in his *History and Antiquities of the Town of Ludlow . (1822)* states categorically that Lucien and the family 'left Ludlow on Sunday June 30, 1811.' Wright is correct. Colonel Leighton warned the Foreign Office on 26 June: 'He leaves Ludlow on Monday next [i.e. the 1 July], it will be a great satisfaction to me to be able to point out his future limits to him before he arrives at Thorngrove.' On 2 July Leighton corrects this statement, 'Lucien Bonaparte took up residence last Sunday evening [30 June].' and reported that Lucien was satisfied with his limits. These limits are not described at this point but we learn later that Lucien was permitted to go to Worcester and could make excursions up to a ten mile limit.

3 July 1811. *The Hereford Journal* reported, in the same edition as the one above, another snippet of information that 'At Ludlow Church, £32 10s 6d has been collected for the benefit of the British prisoners in France.' It was a sizeable sum for a church collection, perhaps worth £1770 in 2012 terms. Perhaps the citizens of Ludlow, feeling a little put out at having lost their celebrity, wished to mark his departure.

6 July 1811. *The Oxford Journal* informed its readers 'Lucien Bonaparte is arrived at Thorngrove, near Worcester, with part of his family [had some remained behind at Dinham?] He is accompanied by Colonel Leighton, who attends him by order of Government, and inspects his letters etc.' The *Memoirs* reported that 'Colonel Layton' (sic) examined Lucien's correspondence with 'much more severity and exactness' and went on to describe how 'all letters addressed to the family, were delivered to the Colonel, locked up in a small box, of which the commissary kept a key, and having read them, were forwarded on to Thorngrove. The answers, or any other communications which Lucien might be desirous of sending, also passed through the hands of the above personage.'

3 August 1811. *The Northampton Mercury* brought some fresh news/gossip 'The daughter of Lucien Bonaparte, it is said, is shortly to be married to Mr Charlton, a young man of 24 years of age, and possessing a considerable portion of landed property. The fair foreigner is handsome, and very highly spoken of. Mr Charlton is of the family of Lechmeres.' *The Caledonian Mercury* added on 5 August that 'The match is approved of by all parties, and promises to prove a happy one.' It is not made clear which daughter this is but the eldest Charlotte was nearly sixteen and it was not unusual to be betrothed at such a young age. However, the story seems unlikely to be true. Lucien did not approve and the story is firmly rebutted as evidenced by the following report.

14 August 1811. *The Hereford Journal* stated: 'The report that the daughter of Lucien Bonaparte is going to be married to an English gentleman, named Charlton, has been formally contradicted by the Abbé Charpentier, who belongs to Lucien's domestic establishment'.

One could imagine that Lucien and Alexandrine, if not the whole family, were fervently hoping that the move to Thorngrove would provide some much needed peace and tranquility. There seemed no doubt that they were to remain in England for the foreseeable future and have their freedom of movement restricted. No matter how comfortable they could make their prison it was still a prison and their duty would be to shield their children as much as they could from the consequences by providing as normal a home as possible. Was it to be?

The narrative continues on page 94.

68

COLOUR PLATES

Plastico del forte Michelangelo (Istituto storico e di cultura dell'arma del Genio di Roma)

Fort Michelangelo, Civitavecchia, as Lucien would have seen it. Today the port caters for a fast growing cruise-liner trade.

A copy of *Unconditional Surrender* by Seward Johnson, is a favourite with tourists. © BRS 2012

70

HMS *POMONE,* 38 Gun Frigate, took Lucien to Malta, commanded by Captain Robert Barrie.

Fort Ricasoli at the entrance of Valletta Harbour, Malta. Lucien's prison for four weeks.

Lieutenant General Sir Hildebrand Oakes, GCB Governor of Malta.
Painting attributed to Henry Raeburn. National Trust Collection.

The former Grand Master's house on Malta, St Antonio, to which Lucien moved. with his family for the period September to October 1810.

Three portraits of Christine Boyer (1773-1800)
Lucien Bonaparte's first wife
and mother of 'Lolotte' and 'Lili'.

Above,
C Boyer attributed to
Jean-Baptiste Isabey.
Courtesy of Museo
Napoleonica, Rome.

Below,
C Boyer by Jacques
Sablet, 1799.
Courtesy of Palais Fech, Musée
des beau-arts, Ajaccio.

Above,
C Boyer by Antoine-Jean Gros, 1800.
Courtesy of the Louvre, Paris.

Lucien Bonaparte playing backgammon on board HMS President.
The man behind Lucien. has been identified as Père Maurice by his long nose.

Charles de Châtillon, the artist, curly hair, placed himself in the centre.
The sketch is dated 11 December 1810.

Captain Samuel Warren with Lucien's eight year old son Charles at
his elbow. Other members of the family look on. The man behind
Warren is thought to be André Boyer.

The image is reproduced courtesy of the Museo Napoleonico, Rome.

The ex Papal Palace at Canino purchased by Lucien Bonaparte. The building sits on a rocky prominence and was the heart of the town.

The views show the southern aspect (top), the entrance on the east and the internal courtyard which is currently under redevelopment.

© BRS 2012

Musignano from the north (top), main entrance, and east aspect.

Lucien Bonaparte
by François-Xavier Fabre and probably completed between 1808 and 1810.

Alexandrine Bonaparte
by François Xavier Fabre.

This image is reproduced courtesy of the Museo Napoleonico, Rome.

Mount Edgcumbe, Devon, formerly the seat of the Earls Mount Edgcumbe, and close by the anchorage of Barnpool.

The Kings Arms Hotel, Plymouth.

Lymore, Montgomery.

Admiral Sir Robert Calder,
Port Admiral Plymouth.
Painted by Lemuel Francis Abbot
in 1797.

Lt General Richard England the
senior officer who took Lucien's
parole statement on 21 Dec 1810.
Painted by John Downman in
1806 Image courtesy of Sotheby's.

A walk leading to
Dinham House.
The walls to Ludlow
Castle are on the right.

© BRS 2012

↑ The old Ludlow Market Hall and
Assembly Rooms, demolished 1887. © LHRG.

↓ The Angel Inn where Lucien
spent his first night in Ludlow.

Dinham House

Dinham House was occupied by
Lucien Bonaparte and his family from
1 January 1811 until 30 June 1811.

Thorngrove House

Thorngrove House was occupied by
Lucien Bonaparte and his family from
30 June 1811 until 19 August 1814.

82

The Chapel, Hampton Court, Herefordshire.

A water colour, c 1795 by Joseph Mallord William Turner (1775-1851).

Image courtesy of the Whitworth Art Gallery Manchester University.

Mawley Hall, near Cleobury Mortimer.

In 1810 the home of Sir Walter Blount.

Downton Hall, near Ludlow.

In 1811 the home of Sir Charles Rouse-Boughton.

Morville Hall,
today and
below painted by John
Inigo Richards (1731-
1810) c 1790.

Ashford Hall.

Lymore Lodge, near
Montgomery.
The house was
demolished in 1931.

Lymore, Montgomery

The Gorge at La Badia on the Canino estate.
© BRS 2012

The view above the Gorge at La Badia .

The Gorge at Downton by
Thomas Hearne, c.1785.
Private Collection.

Downton Castle on the Teme; from a sketch by Mrs. Stackhouse Acton.

Downton Castle

by Frances Stackhouse
Acton (Née Knight)
c 1830.

And as it is today.

© BRS 2012

Castel di Badia
part of
Lucien Bonaparte's
Canino estate.

© BRS 2012

Lord Castlereagh
Secretary of State for Foreign Affairs
1812-1822.

Lord Liverpool
Prime Minister 1812-27.

Marquess Wellesley
Secretary of State for Foreign Affairs
1809-1812.

Mr Spencer Perceval
Prime Minister 1809-1812.

Charles de Châtillon.

André Boyer.

Both images courtesy of
the Museo Napoleonico
Rome.

Anna ,16

Jeanne, 12

Charles, 12

Louis-Lucien, 2

Alexandrine, 37

Portrait of the Family of Lucien Bonaparte, 1815
by Jean-Auguste-Dominique Ingres

Paul, 6

In the background
are busts of
Lucien Bonaparte
and
Madame Mère

Christine
(Lili), 17   Letitia, 11   Charlotte (Lolotte), 20

Image courtesy of Harvard Art Museums/Fogg Museum,
bequest of Grenville L Winthrop, 1943.837

Examples of the Paintings in Lucien Bonaparte's Collection.

Portrait of a Young Man by Bronzino Courtesy of Metropolitan Museum of Art, HO Havemeyer Collection, Bequest of Mrs HO Havemeyer, 1929.

An Allegory of Prudence
Titian (about 1550-65)
Photo © The National Gallery,
London.

Madonna of the Candelabra
Raphael (1483-1520)
Courtesy The Walters Art Museum
acquired by Henry Walters 1901.

Palazzo Nuñez, Rome,
on the corner of Via Bocca di
Leone
and Via dei Condotti.
Below the carriage entrance on
Via Bocca di Leone.

© BRS 2012

Below; The Villa Rufinella, Frascati.

The church and mausoleum at Canino
containing the remains of Lucien and
some of his family, with Lucien's
statue outside.

© BRS 2012

The casket holds the
remains of Christine
Boyer, Lucien's first wife.

Lucien's memorial casket at Canino.

Thorngrove House

CHAPTER FIVE: THE THORNGROVE PRISON

The Hampshire Telegraph gave a rather more complete account of the activities at Thorngrove in its report of 19 August 1811:

> Lucien Bonaparte is settled in his new residence near Worcester. The establishment is about fifty in family. All the young Bonapartes have two servants in constant attendance on them, besides a cook and a tutor. About a fortnight ago the whole family were employed in making hay before the house. They used nothing but their hands in throwing it about; and laughed at the English of the neighbourhood, who have a different custom. Lucien appears to be always wrapped in thought and gloom; he moves gracefully to such people as salute him, but never speaks. The latter may be owing to his being almost ignorant of the English Language. Madame is agreeable

and chatty; and very particular in making the young part of her family observe the strictest politeness to strangers. The furniture of the house is a mixture of splendor and meaness; as is the dress of the family in general. Lucien gets the *Moniteur* forwarded to him, and such French papers as are published in England. The inspector of his letters etc goes daily to Thorngrove as the mail comes in. There is very little land attached to the house, and so far from Lucien being an agriculturalist, he does not appear to have any fancy that way. He reads poetry in the fields; and generally walks some distance from the family. The shopkeepers of Worcester have been very assiduous in applying for the custom of the family. Lucien has a range of parole four miles from the house, which includes Worcester.

This report was repeated by *The Hull Packet*, *The Hereford Journal*, *The Lancaster Gazette* and *The Aberdeen Journal*, amongst many others.

Thus on the surface all would appear to have been going smoothly and that both Lucien and his family and Colonel Leighton had been able to settle down quietly in their new lodgings.

The *Memoirs* provide an account of Lucien's habits at this time:

Rising every morning at eight o'clock, he breakfasted with the family at nine, and then retired to a small cottage on his own grounds, within a mile of the house, for the purpose of going on with his poem. This occupation continued till one, though occasionally interrupted by shooting: in these excursions Captain Warren's fowling piece was always preferred. Returning to dinner at two, he would often, if the weather permitted, renew the same amusement till five in the evening, and devote the rest of it to literary pursuits, generally retiring at ten. These occupations, though not immediately in his own house, did not, however, prevent Lucien from participating in all the pleasures of domestic life: the whole family used frequently to visit the cottage, and thus afforded him an agreeable variety and relaxation from severer studies.

The Foreign Office letter books however, show that although no major events took place there was a constant stream of minor matters that required attention over the following months. Even in the first week at Thorngrove

Leighton reported that he had heard that a French General, he called him Le Ferse, in fact it was General Lefèbreve-Desnouëttes, was visiting Malvern, which was within the permitted limits of travel of both parties and he wanted to know whether they were allowed to meet. The response from the Foreign Office is not available but was probably negative as they would not have encouraged any liaison between potential leaders of insurrection. Lefèbreve however seems to have been given considerable latitude on his parole. He was quartered at Cheltenham and permitted to travel to Malvern, presumably to attend the spa there, as often as he wanted. His wife was given permission to travel from France and join him at Cheltenham where he already had servants and an aide de camp.

This leniency seems largely to have stemmed from the Duke of Wellington who encouraged the system of parole for senior officers as it had worked to the advantage of both sides in the past and had led to senior officers being exchanged. As the war progressed fewer exchanges occurred and French officers, frustrated by their sojourn in England, sought to escape in ever greater numbers. A Parliamentary report of 1812 stated that for the year to 5 June 1811, of the 2087 officers on parole 118 had broken parole and 71 had made good their escape. Only a few weeks previously, in April 1811, a General Exelman, a great favourite of Napoleon, and a Colonel Auguste de La Grange had escaped from Chesterfield. It would seem most unlikely that in this political climate Lucien was allowed to meet the general. As we shall see later there was some circumstantial evidence that Madame Lefèbreve may indeed have been involved in a clandestine activity by carrying some letters for Lucien from France.

Much of the rest of July was taken up with resolving issues concerning Lucien's domestic staff. As a result of the findings of the Ludlow Quarter Sessions Lucien informed Leighton that he wished to dismiss Seraphino Varelli and send him home to Italy where he could continue earning his living as an engraver. Leighton, aware that dismissed servants of those persons on parole would be treated as ordinary prisoners of war, asked Lucien to retain Varelli until he could make arrangements. Lucien would not agree and Varelli found himself taken to the Sheriff's Office in Worcester. Clearly Varelli was not considered an average prisoner as one of the Sheriff's officers voluntarily accommodated him at his own home for a while. Meanwhile Colonel Leighton elicited a response from the Transport Office that Varelli was to be handed over to Captain Malton, their agent at Bristol, and then imprisoned at the Depot for Prisoners of War at Stapleton. Although Lucien may have been unmoved at this turn of events someone in the family felt some compassion for the man and was concerned that Varelli was to be locked away with the French prisoners as Father Fortin, the priest at Mawley Hall, was informed. The good Father wrote to Colonel Leighton and asked if anything could be done to get Varelli to Italy where he could give much needed support to his family as he thought 'the case a hard one'.

The last sentence also gives us a good indication that the Roman Catholic community maintained its involvement with Lucien throughout his time in England. Another letter at this time asked permission from Colonel Leighton for Père Maurice to be allowed to say mass at a chapel in Worcester.

Lord Coventry was Lord Lieutenant at the time for Worcestershire. He, like Lord Powis, commanded the Militia, and had been made aware by Colonel Leighton of Lucien's presence in his county in a letter dated 2 July: 'I think it my duty … to report to your Lordship … Mr Lucien Bonaparte has taken up residence …'. Lord Coventry, clearly not content with receiving instructions from a lowly Lieutenant Colonel of militia, chose to write to Lord Castlereagh, Secretary of State for War and the Colonies, for instructions on what was expected of him. Whitehall wrote to the Foreign Office and Lord Wellesley in turn wrote to Lord Coventry confirming that Colonel Leighton would keep him informed of any important matters and that 'it is not desirable that any special notice should be taken either of M Lucien Bonaparte or his family by your Lordship'.[84]

Lucien wrote to his mother in a letter dated 20 August. He complained that he had not heard from her despite his many letters to her 'what cruel hand can take pleasure thus in depriving me of the letters of a mother who is so dear to me? …' He goes on to say 'Not long ago we obtained permission to leave the town of Ludlow where we were subject to much unpleasantness; we are now near the town of Worcester in a pretty countryside, and are much better here; we are all in good health …' He ends by saying 'if it is possible to get justice from the Emperor, beg him on my behalf to work for my exchange. Does he not owe this favour to me, who has left my own country twice to please him?'

In September of 1811 Lucien learned that the French Government had removed his name from the lists of those who held government offices in France. Lucien saw an opportunity here and tried to argue the point, through Leighton, that Lord Wellesley had no reason to hold him any longer as he, Lucien, was no longer the holder of any government position. The appeal seems to have fallen on deaf ears and the letter is not answered. Whilst waiting for the reply Lucien set Colonel Leighton off on another tack and asked him to plead that he (Lucien) should not have to pay the bill for either the assessed taxes on his Thorngrove property or the window tax as he was a prisoner of war. On this matter the Treasury was swift to inform the Foreign Office that Lucien was not entitled to any exemption. The unpleasant task of passing on yet more bad news fell again to Colonel Leighton.

On the streets of London *The Morning Chronicle* of 26 September 1811, misinformed those going to work that:

> Lucien Bonaparte's poem is now in the press [it was not]. It begins thus – "Les soldats Bizantins campent aux pieds des murs;" and treats of the achievements of *Charlemagne*. – The stanza is of the above measure in every verse except one, which is short. Each stanza contains ten lines; there are seventy stanzas to every canto; and the cantos amount in number to twenty two, which makes the whole poem consist of fifteen thousand four hundred verses. Lucien has sold it to Miller; and, ambitious to have it translated into English, he has through the bookseller, made an overture to Mr Campbell, the author of 'the Pleasures of Hope', to undertake it, for a remuneration of £2000.

26 September 1811. Sir Walter Scott indicated in a letter to a Mr Morritt that he had been asked to translate *Charlemagne*, 'which I negatived of course, and that roundly.'[85]

In contradiction to *The Morning Chronicle* report above it is presumably at this point that Miller in fact arranges for a man named the Reverend Maunde to undertake the translation.[86] The Reverend Maunde was the curate at the Kenilworth parish which was the living of Doctor Samuel Butler.[87] Dr Samuel Butler lived in Shrewsbury and was headmaster of Shrewsbury School. According to Butler's biographer, his grandson, another Samuel Butler, Dr Butler had agreed to supervise Maunde's translation. One suspects that Colonel Leighton has had a hand in this as they are both Shrewsbury men and it seems very likely that he had approached Butler for help in recommending someone to undertake the work of translation. Dr Samuel Butler was known to support the idea of Catholic emancipation and his involvement would have been looked upon favourably by Lucien.

On the 27 October Leighton informed Hamilton that Lucien wished to discharge two of his 'upper' female servants and hoped that they would be allowed to return to Italy. Lucien had also asked that Leighton find them a decent residence until the two women could leave England. Lucien was prepared to pay the charge. Leighton gave the names as Giovannici Boniaggi (Leighton was never very good with Italian names; the closest name on the parole document is Gennavieve Bagnet) and Lucia Chiappa - and that the latter had two children. The following week Leighton learned that Madame Boniaggi was 'big with child' and that she couldn't travel. Lucien hoped that they would be allowed to travel separately and that if that was permitted he would ask

Barings to make the arrangements. This was the second occasion that Lucien had refused to allow his departing servants to remain in the family home and it may have pointed to another rift of some scale in his domestic arrangements.

16 October 1811. We see that the Lucien Bonaparte story is still considered interesting enough to be used in advertising. *The Hereford Journal* carried the advertisement for a book *A New Description of the Town of Ludlow ...*' One of the selling points was the line that read: 'The family of LUCIEN BONAPARTE described, his talents and pursuits at Ludlow.' 'Printed and sold by W Felton 3/6.'

At this point in the narrative, i.e. some six months into the forced association between Lucien and Colonel Francis Leighton, we can speculate on their relationship. It would appear to be one that grew from mutual respect into friendship, which might be considered strange at first glance with one being an English career soldier and the other a French politician and poet whose countries were at war. On the other hand the relationship typified the relationships that could exist between the educated men in Europe at this time, provided of course they had the means and the opportunity. Both men were of similar age; Leighton at 39 was the elder by just three years. There is no description or picture of Leighton available; but as an active soldier who had endured and survived the climates of the West Indies and Egypt and who was still riding at 62 we could imagine a fit and robust individual and rather the opposite in physical appearance to Lucien. Madame Junot[88] described Lucien as 'tall' – most descriptions actually put him at five feet four inches – she goes on to describe him, rather cruelly, as 'ill shaped, having limbs like those of a field spider, and a small head ... very near sighted which made him half shut his eyes and stoop his head ... though he was rather plain, he pleased generally. He had very remarkable success with women who were themselves very remarkable.'

Leighton was educated at Shrewsbury School and Rugby (Dr Samuel Butler attended both establishments) and 'acquired an extensive and familiar acquaintance with the Greek and Latin classics, to which he later added some of the modern languages.' We could presume therefore that he could read and speak French and was able to converse widely with Lucien. Lucien's grasp of English seems to have been negligible so he would have relished Leighton's ability to speak his language. Both men were married; Leighton married the Honourable Louisa Anne St Leger of the Irish aristocracy in 1805 and had three young children. Lucien had married Alexandrine, a 'commoner', according to Napoleon, but in fact from a well born royalist family in St Malo. Her four children by Lucien were of a similar age to those of the Leightons.

Despite some reports characterizing Leighton as strict in his duties his persona was one that appealed to others. A report on him by a superior when he was a middle ranking officer in the British Army in Egypt describes a person who 'on no occasion has he ever failed me: he has executed every thing entrusted to him with a degree of sagacity, attention, and activity, which can not be too highly praised … Add to this, that his activity is without bustle, his spirit without noise, his merit, in short, without parade or presumption. …' In his obituary in the *Gentleman's Magazine* it was noted that Leighton 'stood conspicuous as a specimen of an English gentleman' and 'whilst firm and conscientious in the maintenance of his own [Tory] principles and opinions, he most cheerfully conceded to those who differed from him the same privilege he claimed for himself.' The obituary continued with praise for his handling of Lucien 'and the firm and judicious yet gentlemanly manner in which this delicate and (as then considered) important duty was executed … gained him the highest approbation of those in power, whilst at the same time it acquired for him the esteem and respect of those eminent individuals who were for three years intrusted [sic] to his charge.' Lucien was fortunate to have such a 'gaoler' and it is probably Leighton's hand we can see dealing with the press on Lucien's behalf and who brought the report below to Lucien's attention and helped him to address the letter that Lucien wrote subsequently.

17 October 1811. Colonel Leighton told Lucien that HMS *Pomone*, the ship that had captured him off Sardinia, had been wrecked on the rocks at The Needles, Isle of Wight, three days earlier whilst returning from the Mediterranean. The newspapers gave several column inches to describing the circumstances of the wreck, which included the fact that Sir Harford Jones, Ambassador to Persia, had been on board with several Arab stallions as a present for King George III. Happily all the crew, passengers and cargo were saved, including the horses. Recalling the generosity of the crew and their Captain for not seizing his possessions Lucien wrote to Captain Barrie expressing his sympathies at the loss of his ship. A subsequent court martial found that it was the Master of the Ship, as the man responsible for the navigation, who was to blame for the wreck, and Captain Barrie was acquitted.

19 October 1811. *The Ipswich Journal* reported that Lucien Bonaparte appeared in the list of individuals who had taken out a licence to kill game. It was not unusual for the local papers to carry these names but it was certainly out of the ordinary for this event to be noted several hundred of miles away in Ipswich. It was another example of providing the public, and particularly those on the coast nearest to the continent, with an excuse to 'tut' at the liberties being permitted to prisoners of war. The report does give some credence to the description we read earlier in the *Memoirs* of Lucien's typical day. Lucien had 130 acres of land over which to shoot and the lake that lay to the front of the house at Thorngrove would also have provided him with some fine duck shooting.

In November Colonel Leighton reported a new development. A Colonel Macleod had visited Lucien at Thorngrove and had invited him to a *fête* at Cheltenham the following year. Leighton informed the visitor that he thought it unlikely that permission would be granted but he duly passed the request on to the Foreign Office. We learn that the Foreign Office agreed with Leighton and that Macleod was informed that Lucien would not be attending. Macleod's reaction was to write to Whitehall to repeat the request with the added information that the event was to be a celebration to mark the birthday of Princess Charlotte of Wales. Apparently Colonel John Macleod of Colbeck, for that is who the visitor was, celebrated the princess's birthday on 7 January each year at his home at No 9 The Crescent, Cheltenham. On further investigation we discover that the Colonel raised a volunteer Regiment in June 1798, known as The Loyal Macleod or Princess Charlotte of Wales's Fencible Regiment. Princess Charlotte, the only daughter of George, Prince of Wales, was only two years old at the time the regiment was formed but no doubt Colonel Macleod was content with the kudos gained by her association with his regiment. The regiment saw some service in Ireland but was disbanded in 1802. It is clear that on this occasion the Colonel wanted to use the celebrity status of Lucien to enhance his annual gathering to toast and demonstrate his loyalty to the crown and the Princess. The plea to Whitehall made no difference. The negative reply indicated that the matter had been considered at the highest level: 'HRH [The Prince Regent] fully appreciates the laudable motives ... but with great regret finds himself precluded from complying with your request.' This was the first year of the Prince's Regency and therefore of his wielding all the powers of the monarchy. It would seem that the Prince was not about to risk upsetting the *status quo* and allowing any French and Scottish connection to blossom despite all the loyal toasts that were elaborately made at these occasions. A page long report of the previous event in January 1811, produced for 'society' in Cheltenham, indicated in its concluding paragraph the extent of the celebrations that year:

> We can only add to the above account, that the refined and elegant hospitalities, characteristic of the House of Macleod, were never more conspicuously exercised, or more satisfactorily displayed. The Royal Pie was most excellent, and after feasting about 80 persons appeared almost undiminished. The Champagne to sparkle *á l' envi*, and to rival the brilliant flashes of a most splendid show of diamonds, of which the display was as tasty as it was costly. The amiable hostess in this, as in everything else that could charm and gratify, appeared first among the first. The Colonel wore a dress uniform, with the addition of the *plaid*, and occasionally the sword, the envied pledge of favour of his Royal Patroness.

Colonel Leighton reported that there never had been any wish on Lucien's part to go to the party. Lucien was probably more interested in getting his poem published than being used by Colonel Macleod.

6 December 1811. Lord Byron wrote to William Harness: we learn from that letter that Byron went with the Reverend Robert Bland to visit Lucien's publisher to persuade him to give Bland the work for translation; unfortunately Miller was out. Later, on 14 December, Byron wrote to Francis Hodgson: 'I have seen Miller, who will see Bland, but I have no great hopes of his obtaining the translation from the crowd of candidates.'

20 December 1811. *The Times* reported: 'Madame Boggie [sic], late governess to Madame Lucien Bonaparte, with her child, arrived at Plymouth on Monday [16th] from Thorngrove, near Worcester. They are waiting to go on board the first cartel for Morlaix whence they proceed to Italy. It is said she returns in consequence of ill health.'[90] Colonel Leighton was in fact already aware that two days earlier this unfortunate woman had been delayed as The Transport Office Agent at Plymouth was not satisfied that her passport was in order. After the Colonel's intervention she was allowed eventually to proceed across The Channel on the 27 January.

The last event of the year for Leighton to deal with concerns the servant, Francesco Lunadi. He was the house steward at Thorngrove and was now reported missing. The Colonel was obliged to inform the Transport Office, the Alien Office and Bow Street (the Police in London) of the incident and he added the following description of the escapee: 'Aged about 28. 5 foot 7 or 8 inches. Black hair, a little curly. Dark eyes, complexion rather fresh and a very little marked with smallpox. He is a well made, good looking man. He generally wears ear rings. Speaks bad French and a very little English.' The reason for this desertion is still unknown. Perhaps the absence of sun and a yearning for the warmth of Italy was getting to the staff.

The New Year had hardly got going before the newspapers were reporting a new story about Lucien to intrigue their readers. 22 February 1812. The *Lancaster Gazette* reported:

> A Birmingham paper contains the following curious intelligence respecting LUCIEN BONAPARTE, for which it does not vouch, but states it to have been received through a respectable channel. For our own parts we do not believe a word of it. – Monsieur LUCIEN BONAPARTE who with his family reside in the neighbour hood of W.[sic] sent a confidential servant to one of his tradesmen, and informed him that a small parcel

would be sent to his house, directed for Monsieur B -, which, as it would contain jewels, of considerable value, was requested to be left called for. When the box arrived, the tradesman thought it most prudent to inform Colonel - ,who is with the family, of the circumstance, and upon the box being opened, not jewels, but letters partly in French and partly in cipher, were found to be the contents; the whole of which, we understand, have been forwarded to Government.

In the next sentence the paper informed its readers: 'There are it is said 50,000 French prisoners in this country, exclusive of officers; some of them have been [here] since 1803! – In France there are 12,000 of our countrymen prisoners.' This report is repeated by both *The Northampton Mercury* and *The Norfolk Chronicle*. *The Hereford Journal* on 11 March informed us that it was the *Birmingham Herald* that printed the first report and which now had received an anonymous letter from Worcester asking that the report be contradicted; they declined: 'we are not in the habit of paying much attention to anonymous correspondents '. We could speculate that this attempt at manipulating the news may again have come from someone close to Lucien. The overall effect at Thorngrove seems to be a self-imposed curfew as for three weeks in a row Colonel Leighton has nothing to report and it would seem Lucien kept his head down hoping the storm would pass. It was slow to do so.

28 February 1812. Colonel Leighton had clearly had enough of all this speculation and no doubt with the full support of the Foreign Office put out the following rebuttal statement that Lucien '… has formally and officially contradicted the statement in the Birmingham paper.'

This correction did not prove enough and several weeks later on 25 May 1812, *The Caledonian Mercury* reports: 'A Morning paper says 'Some discoveries have recently been made, which render the departure of LUCIEN BONAPARTE from this country a measure of indispensable necessity.' *The Northampton Mercury* repeats the same news on 30 May. *The Lancaster Gazette* chips in on 6 June with the certainty that 'LUCIEN BONAPARTE has been detected in an improper correspondence, and will be sent out of the country.' *The Derby Mercury* on 11 June identified the original source as *The Shrewsbury Chronicle*.

The facts of this matter were known to Lucien, Colonel Leighton and the Foreign Office as early as 2 January. It would appear that General Lefèbreve's wife had indeed approached a Worcester draper by the name of Smith who was asked to deliver a parcel, said to contain a box of jewellry, to Mademoiselle Bonaparte. In return Smith would receive a recommendation to the family, but as a loyal citizen he instead went to Colonel Leighton and reported the approach.

The Colonel opened the parcel to find a letter of recommendation under the outer wrapper and also found within the box another letter, in French, addressed to Lucien's eldest daughter from a person who signed off as 'Binielli'. Colonel Leighton saw that the letter was innocent enough, asking for news of the family. He decided to show Lucien the package and told him how it came into his possession. Lucien informed him that Binielli is Madame Lefèbreve's mother's maiden name and it is on behalf of Lucien's mother that the questions are being asked because Madame Mère was uncertain that her letters were reaching her son. Lucien was concerned that Napoleon did not get to hear that anyone from the family was communicating with him and suggested that the letter be answered through the same channels. Colonel Leighton seems to have relished this bit of intrigue and suggested to Hamilton that they should permit this ruse and indicated that they might learn something. He proposed that he would continue to inspect the letters both to and from any of the correspondents that Mr Smith brought him. Lucien was keen for Colonel Leighton to point out to the Foreign Office that, as far as he was concerned, the content of the letter from Madame Lefèbreve made it clear that there had been no clandestine correspondence with the General or his wife when they visited Malvern.

As was mentioned earlier those prisoners on parole were required to obey the rules. These rules were known to the public and within the parole towns they would even have been posted on notice-boards for all to see. Citizens, like Mr Smith, would have been encouraged to report any transgressions by the prisoners and were even rewarded by magistrates when convictions ensued. The reward was usually of the amount of 10/-, which represented over a week's wage for many. There was therefore some easy money to be made for reporting a parolee if he returned late to his lodgings or for some other forbidden activity. In this case it is likely that Mr Smith was not motivated by financial reward; the thanks of Colonel Leighton were reward enough. The public at this period of the war generally felt more than the usual antipathy towards the French and Colonel Leighton is moved to report that he had been told that a group of French officers were recently moved through Worcester and had caused considerable upset to the locals. The Colonel felt this incident should not be ignored and informed Hamilton that their escorting officer 'was not present'. He clearly felt that someone was in dereliction of their military duty.

Lucien had probably not been caught out trying to smuggle letters in and out of the country. He often complained of not getting mail to or from Italy but it seems unlikely that he would wish to risk closer confinement and the consequent discomfort of his family by upsetting his custodians by engaging in clandestine correspondence. The 'Binielli' incident, as Leighton referred to it, did cause Lucien to remark to Colonel Leighton that he did not believe the parole document had included any sort of restriction on mail, and that if it had he certainly would not have signed it. Rather than argue Leighton asked Hamilton if he could have a copy of the document. This was eventually produced and showed clearly (page 36/37) that Lucien had agreed to the restriction, and had signed the document. Lucien must have had to accept that he was mistaken.

Colonel Leighton considers nothing worthy of report throughout March, April and May of 1812 and we can only conclude that Lucien had decided to remain quietly in the country. It is not very surprising as on the one hand America was about to declare war with Britain and on the other Britain was deeply involved in fighting the French in the Peninsular War at this time. In addition Lucien would have been well aware that closer to home rumours were rife of insurrection amongst the prisoner of war population.

In many of the parole towns it would seem there was widespread abuse of the mail inspection system. This abuse was often with the connivance of those same, British, agents who were required to uphold the law but were willing to accept a bribe, turn a blind eye and allow mail to get out. The passage of information between groups of officers on parole was entirely possible and it was probable that the majority of the newspaper stories of clandestine correspondence in regard to Lucien stemmed not from his activities but rather from the several reports of planned insurrection amongst the French prisoners, such as the one reported to the Transport Office in 1812 and considered so seriously they copied it to the commanders of all prisons:[91]

Extra Secret Intelligence

The large fleet here [Boulogne] remain perfectly inactive, but the Flotilla are only waiting for orders. I was yesterday told by one of the Captains that 6,000 men would soon be embarked, that the place of landing was to be near as possible to Stilton Prison [Norman Cross] and that every man was to carry two complete sets of arms etc, in order to equip the prisoners they may release.

Further intelligence reported by the Transport Office was that three emissaries were due to land in England, gain access to the prisons, and prepare the minds of the inmates for the 'Great Event'.

There were many alarms of this nature. In 1812 it had been reported to parliament that in the previous year 464 officers on parole had escaped. It was not that surprising as there were several known, English, escape 'agents' ready to earn money and arrange the smuggling of escapees back to France. The going rate was £100 for four men. The Transport Office was still smarting at the escape of General Lefèbreve-Desnouëttes earlier in the year. We discovered earlier that he had been paroled in Cheltenham and had permission to travel to Malvern regularly, presumably to take the waters. What we did not know was that when his wife had been permitted to join him in England she had apparently brought a message from Napoleon that the General's return to France would be welcomed. According to the news reports the General, dressed as a Russian Count, Madame dressed in boys' clothes as his son, and the General's aide-de-camp disguised himself as a valet. All went together in a poste-chaise from Cheltenham via London to Dover and took ship for France. This particular escape was reported to have cost the General some £210.[92]

One further account involving General Lefèbreve suggests that Lucien, always short of money, had requested his mother send money to him.[93] It appears that she had arranged for it to be smuggled to General Lefèbreve, in order not to implicate Lucien should the ruse be discovered, and for the General to pass on the 50,000 francs to Lucien. Given that Worcester was 'in bounds' to Lucien and not far from Malvern the story may have some truth but evidence has yet to be found.

On 11 May 1812 Mr Spencer Perceval, the British Prime Minister, was assassinated. Lord Liverpool became Prime Minister and appointed Lord Castlereagh as Secretary of State for Foreign Affairs. Matters regarding the escape of prisoners of war had overall got to such a head in 1812 that Castlereagh proposed in Parliament that to aid a prisoner in his escape should now be a felony punishable by transportation for a minimum of seven years and up to life. It is surprising that up to this point the crime for smuggling prisoners out of the country was considered only a misdemeanour.

On 1 June 1812 a letter was sent by Colonel Leighton, addressed from Ludlow, in response to one from Dr Butler who had presumably questioned the reports of suspicious letters.[94] Colonel Leighton replied, 'I am as much in the dark with respect to the cause of the increased suspicion of Monsieur Lucien Bonaparte as yourself, but that I fancy from the nature of my late correspondence with the Foreign Office that representations have been made from some quarter to Government, which it is not thought prudent to disregard.' Dr Butler would have been concerned to know if there had been any 'improper correspondence'. He was after all helping 'the brother of the Tyrant', albeit in a small way, in a commercial enterprise. Should public opinion take against Lucien to any great extent Butler's own reputation and the success of his own school, Shrewsbury School, could have been damaged by this association.

13 June 1812. *The Lancaster Gazette* reports the single sentence: 'Lucien Bonaparte's poem of *Charlemagne*, it is said, has been published on the continent under a feigned name.' It had not.

18 June 1812. The United States declared war on Great Britain.

Lucien was of course alert to the change of Secretaries of State that had occurred in the previous month and saw this as a new opportunity to seek his release. He sent a letter to the new Secretary of State on 26 June asking to be allowed to continue his journey to America. Unfortunately he did not get any more joy from the new Secretary of State than from the last. As it would now seem likely that his stay in England was to be prolonged Lucien knew that he was going to need more funds. He needed to arrange for his assets to be brought to England and sold but these mainly comprised those paintings and works of art that he had left in Rome. He also needed someone he could trust to go and get them. He applied for and got permission to send André Boyer, the nephew who had travelled with him, to Italy and make the necessary arrangements. On 29 June an instruction from Mr Hamilton was sent to a Mr Freeling at Falmouth to direct the Agent of Packets there 'not to give any interruption to Mr Boyer … who is about to embark on board the next Mediterranean packet for Malta – although he may be the bearer of several letters from Lucien Bonaparte and his family to their friends in Italy – these having been already submitted to inspection and Mr Boyer's voyage being sanctioned by the Government.'

The new order at the Foreign Office would appear to have been a little more relaxed under Lord Castlereagh, in relation to Lucien's staff and family at least, if not to his desire to go to America. Leighton responded to the new regime and passed on a request for Madame Lucien to be permitted to take her daughter to visit a convent near Evesham as they were considering placing her there. In the same letter of 16 July Leighton reported that a Mr Lee from the American Legation had visited Lucien and informed him that it was not considered expedient to grant the request to go to America. It is not made clear who considered it 'not expedient' – the Americans or the British. Leighton reported that Lucien had not really absorbed the fact that he was being refused permission to go and talked as if his request to emigrate was still under review. Four days later Leighton reported that the American Ambassador, Mr Russell, had visited Thorngrove but he did not relate what conversation took place.[95] This lack of detail suggested that Colonel Leighton may not have been there when the meeting took place. The Americans had declared war by the time of Mr Russell's visit but he apparently only received notice of this event on 29 July and it was only then that he suspended his official functions.

We now begin to get a picture of an association that Lucien has made with some members of the scientific community in England. Since his sojourn in Ludlow, and the subsequent realization that he was not some sort of ogre, some 'people of quality' had sought out Lucien's company; they tended to be Whigs and usually supported the idea of Catholic emancipation. The Tories on the other hand were still treating Lucien with suspicion and considered his break with Napoleon as a ruse to infiltrate English society. Those who wanted to seek Lucien's company had to visit him, as he was generally unable to travel to them due to the distance restriction. One such family were the Whitmores who lived at Dudmaston Hall, near Bridgnorth in Shropshire, and they were recorded as visiting frequently. Georgiana Whitmore, the daughter, had successfully attracted the attentions of one Charles Babbage who at that time was at Cambridge University with his friend John Herschel.[96] By July 1812 the young Herschel was addressing Babbage as 'Citizen' in his letters, as he recognized the influence Lucien was having on the young mathematician.[97] Lucien was apparently seen by Babbage as a romantic figure: the man who had rejected a kingdom for love, and who represented the best aspects of France. It is from Lucien, it is said, that Babbage acquired a certain militant approach to science as well as some good social connections on the continent. Georgiana's brother, William Wolryche-Whitmore, visited Napoleon whilst he was exiled on Elba in 1814 when on his honeymoon and no doubt brought news back to Thorngrove about his brother. William was to become a major proponent of Parliamentary reform and for Catholic emancipation. One can therefore see how readily a friendship was formed between this family and the Bonaparte family. The friendship with John Herschel led Lucien to a relationship with William Herschel, John's father and famous astronomer. In due course we shall investigate this connection further as it leads to an interesting development.

5 August 1812. *The Hereford Journal* reported: 'Among the subscribers for the relief of the poor at Worcester, of which 1,980 persons participate, appears the name of LUCIEN BONAPARTE, for £50. He has taken a house near the city.' Despite Lucien's reported shortage of funds it is clear that he considered that some largesse was required to counter some of the 'anti' newspaper reports. The subscription was quite timely as it turns out as we see from the next report which followed two days later.

7 August 1812. The *Worcester Journal* stated:

> On Friday one of LUCIEN BONAPARTE's servants, named Luigi Vespasiani, having a trifling dispute with the coachman, was so enraged with him, that, with a knife he stabbed him in the belly. M Lucien immediately discharged the fellow from his service; and as all foreign servants, discharged by him, are considered close prisoners of war, Luigi has been lodged in our city jail till the pleasure of Government is known respecting him. The man who was stabbed is recovering.

Colonel Leighton had of course already informed Hamilton of this incident and from his letter we learn a little more detail. The servant who was wounded was in fact English – this is the first indication we have that Lucien was employing local people. It was not the first time that this particular servant, in fact called Virgini, had attacked others and Lucien was adamant that he wished him to be placed in prison, which on this occasion seemed to suit all concerned.

We could reasonably speculate that Lucien and his family this summer of 1812 would have had the opportunity to explore a little of the countryside around Thorngrove and associate with some of the local families. Just a pleasant walk of some 5 miles away lay Witley Court, a fine house to which John Nash had just completed the construction of an imposing portico. Thomas Foley and his wife Lady Cecilia lived there with their young family. They were of a Whig persuasion and it seems entirely probable that Lucien would have been invited to join the Foleys for walks in their 1000 acre deer park and admire the revamped building. As the illustration shows this was before the landscape had been rearranged into terraces by William Andrews Nesfield circa 1860.

Witley Court c 1810. Unknown artist. Image courtesy of Dudley Museum.

During the same summer months Leighton has had the opportunity to talk to Lucien at some length. He still felt he had the duty to explore the reasons for the split between Lucien and his brother and to report generally on Lucien's thoughts on developments in France. One long letter Leighton sent to the Foreign Office in August sets out Lucien's thoughts, perhaps better described as ramblings, on how Lucien might assist in negotiating a peace between the two countries. The letter from Leighton gets no response. A second letter reporting a two hour conversation with Lucien on politics is treated similarly. A third letter in early September from Leighton reports that he suspects Lucien may be planning to leave England but there are no further details. One might expect that this last letter might have elicited some reaction but increasingly one has to take the view that Lucien's opinions are becoming increasingly irrelevant to the Foreign Office. Later in November the position is made clearer and Hamilton confirms by letter that 'government' is not interested in Lucien's thoughts.

7 September 1812. John Murray wrote to Lord Byron and told him that he had visited Lucien, presumably at Thorngrove, 'to make arrangements for his poem, which, with the translation, will form two volumes in quarto, and which I am to publish immediately, if his brother will permit its circulation on the continent. Lucien is commanding and interesting in his person and address.'[98] This visit is not reported to Hamilton and it probably indicated that Colonel Leighton was now using more discretion concerning what needed to be reported and what did not.

14 September 1812. Lord Byron in a letter to John Murray understood that as Murray was now Lucien's publisher he hoped that Murray could arrange an interview with him now that 'the gods have made him poetical'. Byron had been in the habit of visiting Lady Oxford at Eywood and it would have been relatively easy to make a detour to Thorngrove, only a days' ride away. Neither Byron nor Lucien have mentioned a meeting in their memoirs/biographies and the 'interview' probably did not happen.

In September 1812, Colonel Leighton had a number of requests to pass on to Hamilton. The first was that Lucien's daughter (unnamed but probably Christine) might be ill and the request was for her to travel to London to seek medical advice. Next was a request for the two ex-servants imprisoned at Stapleton to be allowed to go France and then travel onward to Italy. Lastly there was another request from Colonel Macleod who has asked that Lucien's daughters be allowed to visit him at Cheltenham.

The response is swift as far as allowing the visit to London. 'Passports' for the daughter and servants are issued for the period 24 September to 5 October by the Mayor of Worcester. Leighton informed Hamilton that the party will be lodged at an hotel in Berkeley Square. The reply with regard to the servants does not appear to be forthcoming and the request from Colonel Macleod is refused.

November is taken up with an exchange of letters to and from the Treasury. Lucien had been asked to pay the current tax on servants. He questions, not unreasonably we might think, why he should be taxed on those servants no longer in his employment, such as the two in Stapleton Prison. The response from the Treasury is predictable; Lucien is not exempt and is required to pay as they were still considered his servants. The need for the Treasury to raise money for the war effort was paramount and it was in 1812 that the tax was increased for all 'non-essential' servants such as butlers, footmen and valets etc. The rate for male servants, in households that had more than eleven servants, was £7 13s for each. Should those servants have been required to wear powdered wigs there would have been a further levy.[99] The tax on hair powder for wigs was not repealed until 1869. Colonel Leighton reported that Lucien 'says he will part with most if not all [his servants] in consequence.'

On 15 December Colonel Leighton enquired on Lucien's behalf if the Foreign Office was holding any letters from Boyer as he had heard nothing from him since he had departed nearly six months earlier in June. The Foreign Office replied that they did not. Later that month Hamilton was informed that a Mr Primus had arrived at Thorngrove bearing letters and a 'petite boite de Diamans' from Madame de la Borde.[100] Leighton said that he thought the box of diamonds were of 'some value'. He also reported that from letters he had seen Lucien had been trying to persuade his mother to approach the French government in order to have him appointed as Commissioner for the Exchange of Prisoners. We can only speculate why he wanted to do this. Perhaps it was an attempt to earn some money. The need for this may have been assuaged somewhat by the news on 31 December, as reported by Leighton, that the 'House of Caze-nnove [sic] has advised Lucien Bonaparte that a credit of £1850 has been given to him at their bank by one of their correspondents in Paris – but the name is not mentioned'. Perhaps it came from his mother. This not inconsiderable sum, perhaps approaching £100,000 in todays terms, must have been welcome, particularly as Alexandrine was about to enlarge the family with another child.

4 January 1813. We learn from various notices posted in both newspapers and the *Gentleman's Magazine* that 'Madame LUCIEN BONAPARTE, has given birth to a son'. No further details are given but other sources tell us that this is the birth of Louis Lucien Bonaparte and that he was baptized the following day at Mawley Hall, near Cleobury Mortimer, Shropshire, at the Chapel of St Mary's (since demolished).[101] He was baptized by Dennis Fortin, the priest who lived at Mawley and who styled himself Missionary of the Congregation of Mawley. Charles Jules Lawrence Lucien Bonaparte (sic) 'brother to the infant', aged 10, was named as the godfather and 18 year old Charlotte Bonaparte, 'sister of the same infant, born at St Maximin, in Provence in France' was named as the god-mother. We can perhaps assume that as there were no others named the occasion was wholly a family affair. Interestingly a version of Alexandrine's full name is given in an Anglicized form in the register as 'Mary Alexandrine Charlotte Louise Lawrence, of Bleschamp, born at Calais in France'.

Mawley Hall, as a note to remind readers, was the home of Sir Edward and Lady Mary Blount (1795-1881).[102] The private chapel at Mawley was not the closest for the Bonapartes to reach as there were others in Worcester and Mawley lies some 17 miles to the north of Thorngrove. The choice of venue would appear to indicate that there had developed a bond of friendship between the two families. Had it been otherwise it would have made more sense for the priest to visit Thorngrove for the baptism and not require Alexandrine to make what must have been an uncomfortable journey the day after the birth.

They may have stayed the night at Mawley Hall or perhaps even two. Staying the night away was not in fact a permitted activity by the rules of parole but we are beginning to suspect that some licence or at least a blind eye is being permitted by Colonel Leighton to local visits by Lucien. Any stay could not have been much longer, as there is a report that the Duke of Norfolk visited Thorngrove on 7 January. As he was from one of England's leading Catholic families his purpose was most likely to congratulate the parents on their new arrival whilst on his way home to Arundel Castle. He was now in late middle age and an over large individual who may well have been visiting his long time friends the Oxfords at Eywood, not far from Thorngrove.

The news that Napoleon's march on Moscow had ended in defeat prompted Lucien to offer his services again, through Colonel Leighton, to negotiate peace with his brother. Again there was no response from government.

In March Leighton received a letter from Lord Castlereagh who related that he had received an anonymous letter which alleged that there was a 'great danger of intimacy' between Colonel Macleod of Colbeck and Lucien. Lord Castlereagh said that he was extremely unwilling to believe it but wished Leighton to let Lucien know of the accusation. Leighton quickly responded in defence of Lucien and stated that there was no intimacy and that he had received merely one letter from him and that congratulated him on the birth of his son. Lucien positively denied the charge of any intimacy.

Later the same month Leighton reported that Reverend Maunde intended to spend 3-4 days at Thorngrove. Leighton described him as a most 'respectable and honourable man' and suggested that it was an ideal time for him (Leighton) to conduct some personal business and he requested four days leave following Maunde's expected arrival on 21 April. The next letter, dated 23 April, showed that things had not gone according to plan. 'I have not gone. Maunde is in such a state of ill-health. He could not leave his inn – he died this morning.'

27 April 1813. *The Gentleman's Magazine* and later *The Sussex Advertiser* on 22 May reported a little more detail than that which Leighton had given: 'At Worcester died Rev John Maunde, 43, curate of Kenilworth, on his way to take

up with the living of Abberton, Evesham, at the time of his death of a violent fit of coughing at the Crown Inn Worcester, he was engaged by Lucien Bonaparte to translate into English his poem, he had advanced as far as the 8th canto.'

It is probable that shortly after this sad news was received Dr Samuel Butler met Lucien, if he had not done so already, to discuss the continuation of the translation of *Charlemagne*. Thorngrove is 50 miles from Shrewsbury and it would have been expected that Butler would stay the night. It is quite likely that the invitation to do so sprang more from a desire to converse with a fellow academic rather than merely playing the part of a good host. Butler recalled in a later note for his memoirs that Lucien showed him his medal cabinet and that he was amused to see amongst the medals, wraps of paper, each containing a sweet, Lucien apparently explaining 'C'est pour les enfants'. That evening Butler was treated to a performance of the pantomime *Pylades and Orestes* put on by Lucien's children. 'Later Mademoiselle Bonaparte played the part of Nausicaa in the pantomimic shipwreck of Ulysses, and sang me a little Greek song.' Dr Butler by all accounts got on well with Lucien and became a friend of the whole family. When Lucien and he corresponded they did so in French. Presumably Dr Butler spoke the language well enough to maintain conversation, as we know that Lucien still had very little English; but we suspect that Madame had a better grasp of the language.

12 May 1813. *The Hereford Journal* now chose to place a very pro-Lucien article in its pages. The article goes over some old ground recounting how it was that Lucien broke with his brother. The principal theme was that of Lucien remonstrating with his brother in 1804 when he, and then his mother, failed to plead successfully for the life of Duc d'Enghien who was charged with treason and swiftly executed on Napoleon's orders. Lucien was quoted as saying 'I quit France for I will not live under a man who disgraces himself at once as a son by his want of affection, and as a man by his cruelty. You will render everyman your enemy…' Yet again this article would seem to have been 'placed' by some-one close to Lucien if not at his instigation. The situation on the continent remained uncertain and Lucien may have been concerned to be seen more favourably by the British; not only had his enlarged family every possibility of having to remain in England for the foreseeable future but also he must have hoped for a favourable reception for the publication of his poem.

A curious letter was forwarded on 25 May to Lucien, via the Foreign office, from the French Minister of War. It concerned the permission given by the French to Colonel Macleod to go to France. Macleod apparently had asked to use Lucien's old residence in Paris, the former Hotel de Brienne. Lucien was clearly surprised at this turn of events and denied all knowledge of Macleod's intentions. In any case the residence was no longer Lucien's as it had been sold to his mother in 1806.

On the 11 June 1813 Lucien had to request that his daughter, Christine, be allowed to go to London again and this time he asked for Monsieur de France, the family physician, to accompany her. Again a swift and positive reply was received. We learn later that Christine left for London on the 18th and that 'a surgeon of this town [Worcester]', instead of M de France, was in attendance.

We are reminded in the same letter that Luigi Virgini still lingered in prison. Leighton was told that his family believed that he had been moved and that they had asked where so that they might continue to send him money. A week later the Transport Office informed Leighton that Luigi has not been moved but remained in Stapleton prison. One could suppose it would not be the first time that letters and parcels failed to get past the prison guards, particularly if they contained money. On another subject Leighton reported that Mr Boyer had been in touch with Lucien and was concerned that he not been able to get hold of any of Lucien's effects.

For most of the day of 21 July 1813 Colonel Leighton must have sat at his desk composing a long letter to The Foreign Office. He started rather forlornly by saying that as Hamilton had not had the time to hear his verbal report when he recently visited London he thought it pertinent to set it out in a letter. He then gave yet another lengthy discourse on the thoughts of Lucien Bonaparte. Hamilton was not impressed. There is no sign on the letter in the archive that it had been seen by the Secretary of State in the manner that previous communications were often marked. Hamilton has instead scribbled 'Opinions of LB' as if he had mentally consigned the letter to the wastepaper basket. The Foreign Office had other, more important, matters on their mind. Sir Arthur Wellesley, later the Duke of Wellington, with the combined armies of Spain and Portugal, in addition to his own, had driven the French forces out of the Iberian Peninsula and back over the Pyrenees. An armistice had then been declared as the belligerents attempted to recover from their massive loss of manpower. The Foreign Office was deeply concerned with persuading the Austrians to join the Coalition with their 300,000 troops before hostilities recommenced. It was absolutely the wrong moment for Colonel Leighton to try and get their attention.

Another individual trying to get attention was Seraphino Varelli, Lucien's dismissed engraver. A letter dated July arrived at Thorngrove on 23 August 1813. It was sent from Stapleton Prison to Alexandrine and contains a desperate plea for her to try and arrange 'passports' for his removal to Italy from the 'unhappy situation' in which he finds himself. The letter marked the second anniversary of his incarceration.

On 22 August 1813 we get a further glimpse of the literary world's interest in *Charlemagne:* Lord Byron adds in a postscript to a letter to Thomas Moore; 'I hope you are going on with your grand coup – pray do – or that damned

Lucien Buonaparte will beat us all.[103] I have seen much of his poem in MS, and he really surpasses everything beneath Tasso.[104] Hodgson is translating him against another bard. You and (I believe, Rogers) Scott, Gifford and myself, are to be referred to as judges between the twain, - that is, if you accept the office. Conceive our different opinions! I think we, most of us (I am talking very impudently you will think – us indeed!) have a way of our own, - at least, you and Scott certainly have.'

At the end of August we are reminded that Colonel Leighton still has responsibility for his regiment, The Shrewsbury Volunteers. They are due to assemble at Ludlow on 27 September for two weeks of training and he asks Hamilton to obtain the Secretary of State's permission to attend. As hostilities have recommenced on the continent there was no argument from the Foreign Office and Leighton made arrangements for a 'trusted individual' to stand in for him and to make the visits to Thorngrove but does not tells us who this was.

Then on 10 September Colonel Leighton wrote to Hamilton 'A severe domestic affliction has happened to me in a very sudden manner and has prevented me from paying my accustomed visits at Thorngrove since Tuesday last'; he does not say what this affliction was but reassures Hamilton that 'the family however have been visited by a confidential friend'. He also added that Lucien has heard from Boyer who is on his way with 'the gallery' and other 'objects of art'.

Nine days later a friend (name unreadable) of Colonel Leighton's wrote to Hamilton; 'It is with much concern that I have to inform you of the present distressed state of mind under which Col. Leighton is suffering….' He went on to explain that Leighton's eldest son was ill and was expected to die shortly and at the same time that his wife was due to give birth. 'Col. Leighton begs me to say it will not be in his power to attend to his duty at Thorngrove at present, … '. The tone of the letter very much reflects Leighton's desire to indicate that he wishes to continue with the work. He would not wish to give up his £500 a year and revert to his half pay, which at his rank would be about 8s 6d a day. It was not until Leighton wrote again on 2 October that he finally told Hamilton that his problem was that his father had died and almost at the same time as his son. He requested some leave to go to Yorkshire to clear up his father's affairs. He departed on 5 October and with a remarkable sense of duty was back in harness at Thorngrove eight days later.

20 October 1813. Francis Hodgson received a letter from Lucien (in French) which informs us that he has received Hodgson's rendering of *Juvenale*, and that, although he (Lucien) was no judge of English poetry, he felt public opinion of his (Hodgson's) work was a positive endorsement of the work Hodgson was doing for Lucien on *Charlemagne*.[105] He also informed Hodgson he

had made changes to the 10th canto; all of which confirmed that Hodgson had been working on the translation of *Charlemagne* for some time and probably since April when Maunde died.

On the same day Lord Byron wrote to Samuel Butler, who had apparently asked for an appreciation of Hodgson's talents, and referred to Lucien's poem; 'The little that I have seen by stealth and accident of *Charlemagne* quite electrified me. It must be a stupendous work – it seems to be of another age, … M Lucien will occupy the same space in the annals of poetry which his imperial brother has secured in those of history – except that with posterity the verdict must be in his favour.'

On 21 October Colonel Leighton was able to report that Boyer had arrived in the Thames at Gravesend aboard the ship *Magnet* but apparently 'without having accomplished the main object of his voyage; viz the gallery'. One would expect that Lucien was not too delighted to hear that news. The following week, on 26 October, a letter from Boyer arrived, written from Sandgate Creek, in which Boyer hoped that he would be released from quarantine in 15 days time. He eventually arrived at Thorngrove on 1 December only to be told by Lucien that he wanted him to go to Germany.

26 October 1813. Madame De Stael, writer and poet, wrote to John Murray, her publisher, from Bowood, near Calne in Wiltshire, and asked him to send a copy of her work to Lucien amongst others.[106]

18 December 1813. *The Morning Chronicle* printed a long letter, a column and a half, from a person using the pseudonym, 'CYNEAS', of which this is a small extract:

> It happens by a very extraordinary concurrence of circumstances, that were Napoleon to fall, the two principal claimants to the crown of France, under both order of things, are now in England. Namely Lewis [sic] XVIII, and LUCIEN BONAPARTE. Thus it would be in the power of this Government to offer to France a monarch from either family she might prefer. … Indeed I have never been able to persuade myself, that the motive for detaining Lucien in this country could have been prompted by any other consideration … And it strikes me forcibly, that therefore our present conduct towards Lucien, is in the highest degree absurd ... The making of Lucien in some measure our friend, would perhaps be to ensure a very efficient agent towards peace.

Perhaps detecting some degree of support for the views expressed *The Morning Chronicle* sent a correspondent to Thorngrove to write the 'follow up' piece published a week later.

27 December 1813. *The Morning Chronicle* article, on page 4, is headed:

LUCIEN BONAPARTE

The residence of this estimable brother of the tyrant Bonaparte, near Worcester, is distinguished by various features of magnificence, that may be denominated princely. He has not less than thirty persons who reside with him *en famille*, on terms of friendship, most of whom contribute to the general amusements of this *chateau*, by their skilful performance on various instruments, so that an excellent band of music is daily formed. He has three daughters, who are highly accomplished in singing, dancing, and painting, and who are also excellent actresses. An elegant theatre is tastefully fitted up with all the requisite decorations, in one wing of the house, in which French and Italian pieces are performed in three evenings of the week, several of which are of Lucien's own composition. Two tables, plenteously covered, are well served daily by an appropriate suite of domestics. Lucien and his daughters are visited and received by several of the most distinguished families around. They have permission to resort to any place within ten miles of their place of residence; but their correspondence is subject to the minute inspection of Colonel Leighton stationed at Worcester, and who examines every letter that they receive, or transmit. Lucien makes no secret of the cause of separation from his tyrannic brother. It arose from his forming one of the Military Council that December against the murder of the Duke D'Enghein by an acquittal, on which Napoleon instantly summoned another council, which voted his death. Lucien anticipated the personal consequence to himself, and immediately absconded, just in time to evade the order for his arrest, which arrived a few hours after. He speaks with a grateful feeling on the humane liberality of the British seamen, who on his capture, coming from America [sic] to England, restored to him his jewels and specie to the amount of £80,000. His grand Epic Poem of *Charlemagne* is expected to appear in the course of the next month;

twelve books of which, we understand, are already translated by Mr Hodgson and his literary colleague, at
Cambridge.

This advance publicity, at no cost, must have been very welcome to Lucien.

It is probably about this time that a sculptor, Peter Rouw, was commissioned to carve a relief of Lucien.[107] The relief, in tinted wax, is now in the
Victoria and Albert Museum and was probably created at Lucien's request and
in anticipation of his increased celebrity following the expected launch of
Charlemagne. These reliefs were relatively cheap to reproduce and were often
given as gifts. Rouw's standard price for producing one was 10 guineas and
presumably he would have been paid travelling expenses in addition for his
journey from London to Thorngrove.

Lucien Bonaparte
by
Peter Rouw

Victoria & Albert
Museum

The year ends with Lucien falling ill. Colonel Leighton reported that he
had not seen Lucien at all as he had taken to his bed for four days with a
fever. The New Year started inauspiciously with suggestions of intrigue. Lord
Sidmouth, the Home Secretary, wrote to the Foreign Office, on 25 January 1814,
with the intelligence that 'an alien of suspicious character named Count Bagnoni,
who has recently resided at Cheltenham, has been engaged in correspondence
with Lucien Bonaparte ... ' Colonel Leighton was instructed by the Foreign
Office to 'endeavour to ascertain both the fact and the nature of this correspondence, and forward the result with the least possible delay.' Regrettably there is
no further correspondence on this matter. We can only conclude that
Cheltenham is a hotbed of intrigue and contains several individuals the government needs to keep their eye on.

At the end of January André Boyer is dispatched to London to obtain passports for himself and two servants to travel to Holland and on to Germany; at this stage we do not know why. The arrangements are made through the Baring Brothers bank.

On the continent of Europe the news of 14 February 1814 was that Coalition forces under General Blücher were advancing on Paris. It must now have seemed clear to most people that the end was in sight for Napoleon, although he appeared not to recognize this and fought on. On the same day Lucien requested, through Colonel Leighton, that the two servants in Stapleton Prison should be released. One of them was apparently sick and Lucien 'begs to point out that they are Romans' and asked that they be allowed to return to their country. Hamilton was also informed that Boyer had arrived in Rotterdam and was proceeding to Cologne.

3 March 1814. Many papers included the small snippet of news that; 'LUCIEN BONAPARTE, of Thorngrove House, continues in his state of seclusion, he drives about in a neat one horse chaise, on the panels of which is inscribed a plain and simple 'B'.'

6 March 1814. Lucien addressed a letter direct to the Prime Minister, Lord Liverpool to request his own release:

> To His Excellency ['s attention?] the Count of Liverpool
> Prime Minister of the King of Britain
>
> My Lord
>
> The circumstances which obliged me, 4 years ago, to leave the Roman States to seek asylum in America having just changed through the outcome of the war, I accept today the offer I had been made at the time of my arrest to send me back to the port from which I left, and I ask for the permission to embark with my family to go to Holland in order to return to my home in Italy.
>
> I ask your Excellency to kindly act as the instrument of my request and to extend to me his kind offices for its successful outcome. I would like to hope that my conduct throughout the time of my captivity in this country has caused no displeasure to the British Govern-

ment, and that he will not deny me the justified request that I am addressing to him.

I ask Your Excellency to accept the assurance of the very high consideration with which I have the honour to be

Yours [illegible] ,Lucien Bonaparte

10 March 1814. It is at this time when the news of the advance on Paris has become known that Lucien decides to throw a party. Was this to demonstrate his independence from Napoleon to his English friends or was it a farewell party to thank them for their hospitality as he now anticipated his imprisonment coming to an end? *The Morning Chronicle* reported:

> Thorngrove, The residence of LUCIEN BONAPARTE. On Monday se'night a masked ball was announced and at eight o'clock the doors of this beautiful villa were opened to friends of its hospitable and charming owner. The apartments on the left of the hall to the conservatory were selected and arranged for the occasion; it was a *coup d'oeil* of enchantment, presenting an animated sketch of the scenery of a Venetian carnival. The number of *invites* was less than a hundred, but the masks being changed during the evening, a great variety of novel characters were brought on the stage. LUCIEN BONAPARTE appeared as a Roman peasant; Madame and three of her daughters, as a Tyrolean mother and children, formed a beautiful and interesting picture; while the younger branches of the family were charmingly grouped as Neapolitain *bambinos* at their pantomime sports. The gentlemen of Lucien's suite supported many very enter-taining characters. *The* pleasures of the evening were rendered highly *piquant* by the representation of some comic *enterinezzos,* composed by Lucien, and performed by his family, together with several charming *imprevisa-tores*, given by some of the party present.

It would have been interesting to know who the '*invites*' were. The occasion undoubtedly has the air of a grand farewell party. Lucien was sure in his own mind that he was going home despite not having heard from Lord Liverpool and this must have been a genuine 'thank you' for all those who had offered them hospitality.

17 March 1814. Colonel Leighton wrote that Lucien has heard that Boyer has reached Cologne and that he received attention from the 'Crown Prince of the Swedes' (why was not made clear) and was proceeding to Frankfort (sic) to make arrangements for the publication of *Charlemagne* and obtaining a passport from the Austrian Minister in the hope of getting to Rome and securing Lucien's 'gallery'.

A letter from the Admiralty to the Foreign Office of 21 March indicated that all concerned had reacted swiftly to Lucien's request, in mid February, for the release of his two servants. The Admiralty informed the Secretary of State that they had directed the Transport Board 'to release these two prisoners (Seraphino Varelli and Luigi Virgini) and to send them to Italy by the first opportunity'.

30 March 1814. The Coalition armies defeated Napoleon's forces at the Battle of Montmartre and then entered Paris on the following day - the war was effectively over. Would this circumstance signal Lucien's release?

Napoleon withdrawing after the Battle of Laon 10 March 1814.
By Jean-Louis-Ernest Meissonier. Image courtesy Musée d'Orsay.

CHAPTER SIX: RELEASE

4 April 1814.   *The Hampshire Telegraph* was the first to note: 'LUCIEN BONAPARTE has obtained leave to take up his residence again at Rome. His seat near Worcester is offered for sale.' *The Oxford Journal* repeats the story on 5 April. This report seems to be pure speculation and is proof that government offices in 1814 were as prone to leak information as they are now. It is certainly true that Lucien had requested his release but it was not until 30 April, some three weeks later, that any formal decision was announced.

11 April 1814.   Napoleon Bonaparte abdicated and Louis XVIII, the Bourbon King, put his brother, Charles Comte d'Artois in charge until he could return to France later in May.

12 April 1814. *The Morning Post* noted correctly, though again from leaked information, that permission for his release had been sought by Lucien and granted, before any information 'of the late events' had been received, i.e. that peace was declared and Bonaparte had departed for Elba and exile. It was not clear what point the paper wanted to make other than to demonstrate it had access to privileged information.

A letter from Colonel Leighton, dated 19 April 1814, informed Hamilton: 'that it will be the wish, in a few days, of Mr Lucien Bonaparte to send his daughter [Christine] to Leicestershire for the purpose of being put under the care of Mr Cheshire at Hinckley [the correct spelling is Chessher]. I believe also that it is his wish that two of his female servants should remain with her there, and that one of the gentlemen of the family should accompany her for protection on the road, but the latter should return. The complaint of the young lady is a tendency to deformity, it is, I know the wish of the family that the circumstance shall not be made known; even I am supposed to be ignorant of it '.

Two days later Leighton writes to say: 'As I imagined, Lucien Bonaparte, expressed a wish that the indulgence, which I alluded to in my last letter, should be granted again. Madame Bonaparte, who wishes to accompany the daughter to see her placed under Mr Cheshire's care, has also expressed a desire that I should accompany the party as a protection on the road: a request with which I have every inclination to comply, unless I shall receive a notification from you that there is any objection to my doing so. They propose to set out on the 25th and to return to their residence at Thorngrove on the 26th instant, leaving only the patient and her maid servant, by accompanying them I will probably render passports unnecessary.' Mr Robert Chessher was a nationally renowned surgeon. It is known that in 1810 he had under his care some 200 patients, mostly children in and around his home. He also maintained a workshop at his home for making the splints and braces he needed.[108]

25 April 1814. *The Hampshire Telegraph* reported; 'LUCIEN BONAPARTE, it is said, has foregone his intention of taking up his future residence in Rome: he still remains at [his] Worcestershire villa, with his family.' Other papers, such as *The Hereford Journal* on 27 April and *The Royal Cornwall Gazette* on 30 April pick up the same story. The newspapers are correct in stating that Lucien remained at Thorngrove; if not in the other details.

Colonel Leighton wrote on 25 April to inform Hamilton that Monsieur Châtillon, who was still acting as Lucien's secretary, had applied for a passport to return to France. It would appear that despite having loyally shared a long journey and suffered imprisonment with Lucien the time has come for him to return to France. This is not an option open to Lucien and Châtillon has had to make a choice: loyalty to Lucien and banishment in Rome or loyalty to the Bourbon King and home to France. We could expect that the decision would have been understood by Lucien. Leighton also reported that he expected Lucien to reapply for permission to depart but not with the whole family. He would like them to stay for a few more months. Leighton asked for Hamilton's guidance and instructions.

Two days later Leighton wrote again to say that Lucien had received a letter from 'an agent at Paris' which had made him more 'pressing for his departure'. Clearly events on the continent were moving quickly and Lucien wanted to be ahead of the game. He was not going to be able to return to Italy by travelling through France and would have to find another route.

At last the official position was clarified in a letter from Mr Hamilton to Colonel Leighton, a copy of which was dated 30 April 1814:

> I have great satisfaction in being enabled at length to have it in my power to authorize you by command of the Earl of Liverpool to acquaint Mr Lucien Bonaparte, that he and his family are released from their Parole, and that they are no longer considered as Prisoners of War. – I shall be most happy to give my assistance in promoting any wishes M Lucien Bonaparte may entertain respecting his departure from England – and will thank you to let me know them as early as you please.
>
> Yours truly (signed) Wm Hamilton.

Colonel Leighton wrote back the same day with Lucien's wishes which are little changed from the first thoughts that he had expressed. He confirmed that he would leave the ladies and children at Thorngrove for three or four months and that he would travel with the priest, Père Maurice and one servant, Luigi Alleguini. Leighton added:

> The first use which he intends to make of the restoration of his liberty, is to set off this night, and to visit the residence of Mr Herschel, near Windsor, … he will send the priest to wait upon you for his passports, whom I have provided with a letter to be presented by him to you. His device of keeping his departure secret you will perceive from his letter. He has requested me to express his hope that no objection will be raised to his return to this country for the purpose of fetching the remainder of his family in September.

Leighton also wrote that Châtillon will 'quit the residence' as soon as he received his papers. Leighton stated that he fancied that he would no longer be required shortly and that his function would cease; he reassured Hamilton that he 'shall not quit this place, until I have received further instruction from you'. Colonel Leighton then added in a post script; 'PS Mr L.B. intends to avoid London entirely, and to wait near the residence of Mr Herschel (the astronomer) the return of Père Maurice with his passports; and proceed directly to Harwich, where he means to go to Holland in a packet.'

The above postscript poses for the reader rather more questions than it provides explanation. When did Lucien become interested in astronomy? It is more than likely that he had commenced an interest much earlier than his meetings with John Herschel. We know that William Herschel had been asked to provide a telescope for the King of Spain during that period when Lucien was ambassador there and it may well have been a topic of conversation.[109] Père Maurice, Lucien's household priest and tutor, was an extremely knowledgeable individual and as well as teaching the children in many subjects one suspects he was instrumental in advancing Lucien's knowledge and interest in the stars. We discover later that an observatory is included in the particulars for the sale of Thorngrove and it would seem likely that Père Maurice had already formed a relationship with Herschel even if Lucien had not. Most of the subsequent correspondence between Herschel and Lucien passes on compliments to and from 'Rev Père Maurice'. However, apart from Colonel Leighton's postscript the first firm indication of Lucien's interest is the letter Lucien writes from Harwich which is dated 6 May 1814. It coincidentally confirms that Lucien has left Thorngrove and is on his way to Rome.

In the letter, written in French, Lucien regrets that he can not return to Herschel's house and resume the *'intéressante conversation'* that they had some days ago when Lucien spoke of his wish to acquire mirrors for a large telescope 'exactly the same as the one through which you showed me the satellites of … [here he uses a symbol which may be Herschel's symbol for a planet]'. So begins a lengthy and at times very detailed and technical correspondence on the purchase, erection and usage of telescopes which continues certainly until 1816 after which the archives of the Royal Astronomical Society hold no further references to Lucien. [110] The letter also clearly indicates that Lucien has, certainly during the latter stages of his imprisonment, travelled well outside his bounds. The visit does not appear to have been recorded by Herschel or his daughter, perhaps they were asked not to.

Also on 6 May Leighton reported to Hamilton: ' … the departure of my principal charge … '. He reported that M Châtillon had gone to London on behalf of family business and that another servant had asked to go to Oswestry to join others on parole that were being returned to France. He also mentioned that Luigi Virgini, the erstwhile prisoner at Stapleton, had asked to occupy a property close to Thorngrove and then move back to Italy with the family. Colonel Leighton added to his letter a list of all those of the family who remained in England; Madame Bonaparte, Mademoiselles, Charlotte, Christine, Anna, Letitia, Jeanne; Messieurs, Charles, Paul, Lucio; Messieurs, Charpentier, de France; Men Servants, Ferdinand Darando, Vincent Virgini, Domenico Lanzo, Jean Rocelli, Joseph Drisini and Francio Duoini (these last two are labelled; 'Licensed Aliens'); Female Servants, Marianne Vespanoni, Marguerite Vespanoni, Geneoise Baegnet, Lucia Chiappa.

The list was required to satisfy the bureaucrats; the Foreign Office needed to request the Home Office to issue licences for the family to remain in England as they were no longer prisoners but aliens. On the 11 May Lord Sidmouth, Home Secretary, was pleased to direct that licences be issued accordingly. Colonel Leighton then asked that as he had no requirement to superintend the family he might be allowed the occasional absence to conduct some personal business.

19 May 1814. *The Derby Mercury* repeated a *Worcester Journal* article:

> Last Sunday se'night M LUCIEN BONAPARTE left Thorngrove with the intention of proceeding to Rome without delay. The family still remain at Thorngrove, but it is understood that M Lucien will return to England in September, after which all his family will leave this country with him for Italy. We understand with undoubted authority that M Lucien has already departed:

he leaves England with the entire approbation of Government, who have furnished every facility for the occasion. The whole of the family are now considered at perfect liberty.

20 June 1814. *The Morning Post* and others reported that Lucien had arrived in Rome on 27 May and had an audience with the Pope.

On 27 June Colonel Leighton told Hamilton that Madame Bonaparte had received a letter from her husband in Rome dated 1 June in which he asked for Lord Castlereagh and the British Government to be made aware of the circumstances surrounding his reception in Rome. Colonel Leighton para-phrased the letter:

> Mr Lucien Bonaparte arrived at Rome on 27th May: a quarter of an hour after his arrival at the house of his mother he was sent for by the Pope, who received him with open arms, and gave him public and open demonstrations of his attachment to him and of his esteem for his conduct during the time that they were both victims of the most fervent persecution. The Pope enquired with kindness after Mr L.B's family, who he regretted he had not brought with him: and to whom he commanded him to convey the assurance of his paternal affection. Mr Lucien Bonaparte was instructed in a particular manner to assist on the following day 'dans la chapelle Sestine'[sic] at the ceremony of the Pentecost and had a long conference with the Pope.

Leighton then relates that Lucien has been given the title of a Roman Prince and that his Holiness has conferred on him the right to display the arms of the Holy See at his house and that these marks of distinction have been well received by the nobility in Rome. Leighton ended his letter by reminding Hamilton that he had not drawn his salary since last February and enquired when his salary would cease.

In a further letter of 6 July Colonel Leighton related to Hamilton that Madame Bonaparte intended to go to London for several days. He added that Lucien had given up the idea of returning for the family and that he would send his nephew for that purpose which is proposed for the beginning of September. Colonel Leighton explained Madame has 'induced him' to remain at Worcester as, 'he thought it would be unkind to give a refusal, as she seemed to imagine that my residence near her family would render their stay here during Mr L. B's absence more comfortable.'

6 July 1814. *The Hereford Journal* reported that:

> M. LUCIEN BONAPARTE arrived at Rome on the 27th
> May: a few minutes after his arrival in that city the Pope
> requested the pleasure of seeing him; M Lucien accord-
> ingly waited upon his Holiness, who received him with
> great distinction.   The most distinguished persons in
> Rome afterwards waited upon M Lucien. The Pope has
> declared him a Roman Prince (of Canino). – A singular
> circumstance occurred during M Lucien's journey
> through Switzerland: an old lady who was much
> attached to the English, seeing an English carriage stop at
> the inn, went up to the persons who alighted from it, and
> not knowing who they were, supposed them to be
> Englishmen; she accordingly addressed them in English
> upon various topics; M Lucien answered in as good
> English as he was master of; at length she began to speak
> of politics, and was not sparing in her abuse of Napoleon,
> who she characterized in no very gentle manner, compar-
> ing his conduct with that of his brother Lucien, of whom
> she was a great admirer; 'as you come from England,
> (said she) do you know where Lucien is?' 'I believe (said
> M.L.) he is on his way to Rome' 'Indeed (said the Lady), I
> wish he may pass this way, that I might have the oppor-
> tunity of kissing him!'   At another time Lucien's carriage
> was accidentally surrounded by Cossacks, who imagin-
> ing from his dress that he was a Russian
> Officer, saluted him as such.

25 July 1814.   *The Morning Post* issued the following statement which
included the additional information:

> On his proceeding to make the usual reverence, his
> Holiness received him with open arms, and deeply
> lamented the persecution of which Lucien himself, his
> wife and children, had been so long the victims; a
> persecution, which began at the same time with that of
> the Holy Father, and was inflicted from the same quarter.
> His Holiness applauded the purity and firmness of
> Lucien's principles, which had led him to prefer the wilds
> of America to the degraded Crown his IMPERIAL Broth-
> er wished to force on him; and further, in order to give
> the most prompt, decisive, and public mark of his esteem,
> he created him a Roman Prince, and gave his special

permission and authority, for fixing the arms of the Holy
See on Lucien's palaces, at Rome, Tusculum, etc, which
was immediately done, amidst the acclamations of the
Roman people, to whom LUCIEN himself and his family
had been much endeared, during their residence of eight
years in the States of the Church. All the nobility of
Rome hastened to congratulate the New Prince, who has
been welcomed with every demonstration of attachment,
not only by his tenantry and the inhabitants of Tusculum,
but by the general population of Rome. We understand
that the Princess LUCIEN with her family, are preparing
to quit England, in order to return to Rome.

27 July 1814. *The Hereford Journal* reported that the 'Pope had conferred the
title of Prince, Duke of Musignano, on LUCIEN BONAPARTE.'

5 August 1814. Despite his recent return to 'society' in Rome Lucien is
clearly keen to progress his astronomy. He wrote to William Herschel in
response to an unseen letter of 10 July. Lucien informed him that he is arranging
a 'letter of credit' with Barings for three telescopes. In both this letter and in a
copy of the letter to 'A Baring Esq M P, London', Lucien details again the items
that he wants and the price he is prepared to pay: 100 guineas for the mirrors
required for a 7 foot telescope. 1500 guineas for a 10 foot telescope in the
'Newtoniene' form and 600 guineas for the mirrors to construct a 20 foot telescope.

Of course Alexandrine is not there to raise even an eyebrow at this outlay
on Lucien's hobby. Two thousand two hundred guineas was a considerable
sum, possibly £125,000 today, and one can only surmise that he intended spend-
ing some of the proceeds from the sale of Thorngrove once his family had left,
which he anticipated shortly.

11 August 1814, Colonel Leighton wrote to Mr Hamilton that:

At the request of Madame Bonaparte I write to say that it
is her wish to set out on her departure for Italy on the 20th
of this month: that she will be accompanied by her
children, their tutor and the physician, and foreign male
and female servants, in all amounting to twenty: that her
route will be by Ostend, Brussels, along the Rhine,
Switzerland and the Milanese: She has requested me to
express her hopes that you will be obliging enough to
procure for her passports under the name of Madame
Bellini and her family, and 'de les faire viser' [sic, an en-

dorsement] by ambassadors or envoys of the different states through which she is to pass. As I shall be a good deal importuned about a reply to this letter I will be much obliged if you will cause the receipt of this letter to be acknowledged that I may be enabled to tell them whether they may expect to receive the passports by the time specified. As their baggage will consist simply of wearing apparel, it would be a material convenience if they could procure an order from the custom house to let it be embarked without search.

17 August 1814. *The Hereford Journal* reported in reference to the honours heaped on Lucien Bonaparte: 'The cause of these honours is ascribed to the political and religious opinions of Lucien. The Pope has also accepted the dedication of the epic Poem '*Charlemagne*', and Didcot, the celebrated printer at Paris, has undertaken to publish it.'

It is apparent that Mr Hamilton did not act quickly enough for Madame Bonaparte, who was clearly in a hurry to depart as we can see from Colonel Leighton's letter to Hamilton of 24 August with the news that:

> Madame Lucien Bonaparte and her family quit this place on their return to Italy last Friday [19 August], leaving behind only two foreign servants and two children. As it was of consequence to her, on account of the number and age of the children, to experience as little delay as possible, she addressed herself directly to Lord Sidmouth (Home Secretary), as you did not reply to the request, which she wrote to you through me. His Lordship transmitted to her the necessary passports by return of post.

One can almost detect Leighton's regard for Alexandrine in not putting up with any tardiness and going over the heads of anyone who is slow in doing her bidding.

30 August 1814. *The Morning Post* reported 'The Lady and daughter of LUCIEN BONAPARTE left town [London] on Saturday for France. Their ultimate destination is Rome; Where Lucien has taken up his residence.'

3 September 1814. *The Caledonian Mercury* reported that 'On Saturday the Lady and daughter of LUCIEN BONAPARTE, with a very numerous retinue, passed through Gravesend, on their route to Dover, Whence they embark for the continent, and proceed to Rome.'

15 September 1814. *The Caledonian Mercury* reported that the Paris papers dated 7 September stated that Madame Bonaparte had arrived at Bruge on 31 August. She set out next day for Italy.

16 September 1814. Herschel wrote to Lucien that he had ' … the honour of receiving your Serene Highnesses letter … ' and congratulated him on having seen the 'Satellites of the Georgian Planet' which Herschel tells him makes him, 'as far as he knows', the first man in Italy to have done so. Herschel then provides some detailed mathematical equations in answer to questions that look suspiciously like the work of Père Maurice.[111]

4 October 1814. *The Morning Chronicle* carried the notice:

TO BE SOLD AT AUCTION

> The very valuable effects of M LUCIEN BONAPARTE Prince of Canino, at Thorngrove … on Monday 24th day of October and every following day, except Sunday, till the whole is disposed of:

> The very excellent PROPERTY at Thorngrove, belonging to his Excellency the Prince of Canino. Consisting of the genuine, Fashionable and Elegant FURNITURE, of upwards of Fifty Apartments; rich old pier, chimney, figures, and swing glasses and mirrors, of large dimensions; two sweet toned French piano-fortes, with additional keys, one with four pedals, and three strings to each key; harpsichord by Longman and Broderip, barrel organ, capital billiard table 12 feet by 6 feet, fine prints by distinguished artists, many carved and richly gilt picture frames, valuable and extensive library of English and foreign books, 300 copies of a folio volume of engravings of some of the best pieces in the celebrated collection of paintings belonging to his Excellency, which have been recently conveyed from Italy for exhibition and sale in London, stock of prime, fine flavoured, crusted Port, Champagne, and Madeira wines, 153 bushels of wheat, 10 bushels of barley, 655 lbs of good family cheese, pair dark-brown carriage horses well matched, perfectly temperate and of noble action, powerful gig horse, handsome town-built gig with blue lining, red morocco squabs, lamps, covered head, etc. complete and nearly new, carriage and gig horse harness, bridles, saddles, four pleasure and fishing boats, sixteen single and four double

barrel foreign fowling pieces, on superior principles, foreign air-guns, three officers' marquees, etc, etc – To commence each day at eleven o'clock. The whole of the property will be set forth in catalogues, to be published in due time, and had, price 1s 6d each, at the Auction Mart in London; of Messrs Holl and Son, printers, High Street, Worcester; and at the office of Messrs Robins and Terry, Auctioneers, Birmingham.

Immediately below was the following notice:

The elegant MANSION, fit for the immediate reception of a Family of Distinction, with the Park, Plantations, Waters, Cottages, Lodges, Observatory, Gardens, Graperies, greenhouses, Carriage-Houses, Stables, and farm Lands, called THORNGROVE, to be SOLD by Private Contract – Apply to Mr Gillam, solicitor, Worcester. Thorngrove is four miles from Worcester, on the turnpike road leading from that city to Ludlow.

Later in December a fuller description is provided in an advertisement run in *The Times* throughout December, which notes that:

This truly desirable property comprises, with the Mansion House and pleasure grounds, about 130 acres, of rich arable, upland pasture, orchard, and meadow land. … The shrubberies and gardens are well laid out, and in front of the mansion is an extensive lawn, with a fine piece of water.

With the sale of Thorngrove concluded one might have considered the affair with Lucien closed. One could reasonably expect that having been detained in England Lucien would be happy to remain in Italy and never set foot in the country again. It is clear however, that on the contrary, he thought England could still provide him with several advantages.

CHAPTER SEVEN: A VOLUNTARY RETURN

20 October 1814. Lucien wrote to Dr Butler from Rome: 'I hasten to announce the happy arrival of my wife and children, who ask me to give you their affectionate compliments. I will answer a few of your points'. Lucien then asks for the *Charlemagne* draft publication to be sent as soon as possible and adds that he hopes that Butler will visit them in Rome.

2 November 1814. An advertisement in *The Times* states:

> AMATEURS and COLLECTORS of PICTURES are informed that the fine GALLERY of Prince LUCIEN BONAPARTE is just arrived in this capital to be SOLD in one lot. The above mentioned gallery, consisting of 196 pictures of the best masters of every school, will be shown to those persons only who are desirous of becoming purchasers; for this purpose they are requested to address a letter to the Chevalier Boyer, nephew to Prince Lucien Bonaparte, or to his agent, Mr William Buchanan, 60, Pall Mall.

This is the first time that we are aware that Boyer is using the 'rank' of Chevalier, a formal French award. Another Boyer, one of Napoleon's doctors was awarded the title and is recorded, but André Boyer's award has not been found.

11 November 1814. *The Times* ran an advertisement alerting the public to the publication of *Charlemagne* on 15 November.

15 November 1814. Having seen the advertisement noted above William Herschel opens his letter to Lucien saying 'I have long wished to meet with this work, and shall now soon have the pleasure of perusing it.' The main purpose of the letter was to inform Lucien that he has dismantled the 10 foot telescope and is re-polishing the mirrors and making certain improvements such as placing the structure on rollers so that it may be moved in and out of a shelter. This shelter, he advises, is necessary to preserve the mirrors which would otherwise suffer from changes of temperature and damp air. He promises to send more specific detail and directions for the shelter when the instrument is nearly finished.

On 24 November 1814 Colonel Leighton wrote from Shrewsbury so we presume that he has now left Worcester and moved back home. Several exchanges of letters after Lucien's departure were necessary for Leighton to determine from Hamilton just how long his salary was to continue. He seemed to suggest at one stage that he would have been happy to remain to assist Madame Bonaparte out of friendship but if the Foreign Office were willing to continue his salary until she left he was happy to avail himself of it. The Foreign Office did continue to pay the good Colonel and until November when Leighton wrote: 'I have the honour to advise you that this day, being that on which you notified to me that my salary was to cease, I have drawn for £150.0.0 being the amount now due to me. I have the honour to remain dear Sir, your obliged and faithful servant, FK Leighton.' This letter is the last in the Foreign Office letter books and the last we hear of Colonel Francis Leighton until *The Gentleman's Magazine* included his obituary in their pages and informed us that he lived for a further 21 years until he died of a heart attack in 1835 whilst out riding in Shrewsbury with his daughter.

29 November 1814. *The Times* carried another advertisement 'The fine COLLECTION of PICTURES belonging to the Prince LUCIEN BONAPARTE, are now ready for Sale, at the Gallery, 60, Pall Mall …'.

17 December 1814. Lady Holland wrote from Rome to John Wishaw in London.[112] It was a long and chatty letter that described what is going on and who was there. The letter included this description; 'Lucien Buonaparte, who has added to that illustrious name the title of 'Canino', in order to secure to himself a *pied a terre* in this wide world, is a most interesting person; his appearance is grave, his manners good, and his countenance bears the same grand character of the family. He has just sent me the first six cantos of his poem, which I have not read, but see it is in a most pious strain, calculated to aid the orisons [sic] of his Holiness in his oratory, but it is probably well adapted to his views and the times. His wife is an interesting pretty woman, and they are a pattern of conjugal felicity, so perhaps he did well in renouncing a kingdom to retain her.'

21 December 1814. *The Bury & Norwich Post* reported the publication of *Charlemagne* and included the opinion of an unnamed reviewer; '… the poet is not the same monster of genius that his brother was of power. In the career of fame, he does not risk the success of his reputation by the unlimited extravagance of his pretensions. His muse does not disdain to borrow the conceptions of others or to submit to the rules of art; and the boldest flights of his imagination seldom pass the bounds of a well regulated enthusiasm. *Charlemagne* is the work of a very clever man, rather than that of a great poet; it displays more talent than genius, more ingenuity than invention.'

26 December 1814. *The Caledonian Mercury*, almost alone, gave an account of what the poem was actually about: 'The subject is the deliverance of Rome and the Christian Church by Charlemagne, from a league of twenty potentates,

under Didier, King of the Lombards …' The lack of detail generally provided in the remainder of the press rather suggested that not many had read the poem through. It is for much the same reason that more has not been included in this publication – it is not easy to read even in English! It requires a considerable knowledge of both classical and religious literature to be fully understood. To give readers a flavour of the poem the stanza below was selected at random from the 1540 stanzas and is from the first canto:[113]

XXVIII

The astonished Lombards at the first alarms
Of Holy Wilfred's murder rush to arms.
With thousand cries, that to its inmost seat
The palace shake, tumultuously they meet.
Didier is roused, and hastens to restrain
The bold irruption of the foreign train:
His son pursues his steps with eager stride:
His thronging peers are gathered at his side.
Longin himself the daring outrage blames,
He seeks the Monarch and his succor claims:
Adalgise far before the warrior speeds,
With swift advance, and to the temple leads.

7 February 1815. *The Morning Post* carried the notice: 'PRINCE LUCIEN BONAPARTE's Magnificent Collection of PICTURES is NOW OPEN to the public, and will be sold by Private Contract, at the NEW GALLERY, 60, Pall Mall. Admittance 1s. Descriptive Catalogues 1s 6d. – New Gallery, Pall Mall, adjoining the British Gallery.' The word 'individually' was inserted after the phrase 'Private Contract' in the later notices that ran weekly for the next few months until the last on 5 April. We could speculate that Boyer considered a change of tack in his marketing strategy when nobody had come forward to buy the complete collection.

Boyer was perhaps being rather optimistic in trying to sell the collection complete. It consisted of some 198 paintings. As we shall see later many were of considerable merit, and could have been expected to sell for a small fortune. One Titian alone was expected to raise 750 guineas. It would also appear that once Lucien knew that the collection would not be sold as a whole he withdrew some of the best pictures. This would not have helped Boyer's cause.

26 February 1815. Napoleon escaped from Elba. He landed near Antibes, on the south coast of France on 1 March, and marched on Paris gathering an army about him.

3 March 1815. A further advertisement was placed in *The Times*, presumably to ensure that the following 'letter' was published and not left to the whim of the editor to include:

> TO THE EDITOR OF THE TIMES, Sir, - A report having been circulated, and credited by many of the collectors of pictures in this country, that the collection of my uncle, Prince LUCIEN BONAPARTE, will after a short time, be Sold by Public Sale, in the event of the pictures not finding purchasers by private contract, I now beg to leave publicly to state, through the medium of your paper, that such pictures, as shall remain unsold of this collection, on the 1st of August next, will then be transmitted to Rome from whence they were sent at a moment of uncertainty, and before the affairs of the Continent seemed to promise anything of a fixed or settled appearance, which they have now so happily assumed. I have the honour to be, Sir, Your most obedient servant. C BOYER.

The 'affairs of the Continent' have not yet caught up with Boyer and the reports of Napoleon having escaped Elba and of his landing in France do not appear in the newspapers for another ten days. Chevalier Boyer must have been concerned that people were getting the impression that not many pictures had been sold and were now waiting for the price to drop. We do know that a Mr Charles O'Neil bought at least one painting, *Venus and Adonis* by Domenichino, as he sold it as being from Lucien's collection in 1833. Mr Henry Fulton bought another, *Endymion* by Guercino (sic). The collection was not in fact returned to Italy but remained in London and was available for sale for months. In light of the events that were about to unfold, i.e. the return of war with Napoleon, it was not surprising that few sales of either the pictures or the poem were made.

17 Mar 1815. *The Liverpool Mercury* produced a notice, 'This day is published, *Charlemagne: or the Church Delivered*, an Epic Poem in twenty four Books by Lucien Bonaparte. £4, 4s Trans by Rev Samuel Butler, DD and Rev Francis Hodgson AM'.

20 March 1815. On this date Napoleon reached Paris and it is the date generally recognized as the start of Napoleon's 'The Hundred Days' war.

25 March 1815. The Great European Powers agreed the Treaty of Alliance against Bonaparte and later agreed to advance into France on 1 July. The Seventh Coalition forces, as the armies were known, consisted principally of a British army under the Duke of Wellington and a Prussian army under Blücher. The people of England now knew that very shortly they would have to go back

to war. No one was in the mood to buy anything associated with Napoleon particularly as they now heard that, Lucien, to whom they had given 'refuge', had made his peace with Napoleon and was directly aiding and abetting his latest bid for European domination. It was inexplicable.

10 April 1815. Dr Butler wrote to Monsieur Boyer having heard the news from him that Lucien has had a reconciliation with his brother; 'I cannot express how surprised I am … If this is true we should not count on a second edition … such are the prejudices against the Prince ... but patience, I am English, and I cannot forsake my friends … please assure the Prince of my friendship and sincere respect '.

23 April 1815. The Reverend Francis Hodgson wrote to Dr Butler and expressed his irritation at the reconciliation. He perfectly understood, he wrote, that there was little chance of book sales to the British public now that Lucien had sided with his brother: 'I was sick when I heard of Lucien's adherence.' Hodgson knows that they have misjudged the situation but he consoles himself a little with the thought 'Thank heaven ... foolishness of conduct is not faithlessness of, or to, principle.'

29 May 1815. *The Sussex Advertiser* chose this date of impending war to report this rather old news: 'Miss Christiana [sic] Bonaparte, daughter of Lucien Bonaparte, at present resides at Hinckley, in Leicestershire. She is apparently under no restrictions whatever, but visits whom she pleases, and is accustomed to receive foreign strangers as visitors. Miss Bonaparte is a most accomplished young lady, about 19 years of age, and is a daughter of Lucien's by his first wife.'

30 May 1815. Napoleon was still able to command the loyalty of many Frenchmen and by this date had mobilized nearly 200,000 men and had enough to create his *L'Armée du Nord*. Within a few weeks he was on the northern French border and was preparing to advance north into Belgium. He crossed the border on 15 June with the intention of splitting the coalition forces and defeating each in turn. By the afternoon of 18 June Napoleon had failed to drive the British from their chosen ground at Waterloo and with the arrival of the Prussians, Napoleon accepted defeat as inevitable; and demoralized fled the field of battle. Many of his Generals considered he had given up too early but without a leader they had little choice but to retreat towards Paris. By 21 June Napoleon had reached Paris and the next day he abdicated for the second time.

22 June 1815. *The Caledonian Mercury* stated: 'It was stated not long ago that the daughter of Lucien Bonaparte was residing at Hinckley in Leicestershire. Soon after this circumstance was publicly noticed, three foreigners came to the village and carried off the lady, together with all her effects; and it is supposed

they have embarked for France.' Events had moved faster than anticipated and one can imagine Lucien's panic to get his 'Lili' down to a port and on board ship.

23 Jun 1815. *The Cambridge Chronicle*, 'The regular communication with France is now finally stopped. A vessel, however, sailed for Calais on Sunday, with Lucien Bonaparte's daughter on board, who was left behind by her father to have the advantage of medical advice.'

When news arrived in Paris that Napoleon had been defeated at Waterloo Lucien considered coming back to England. He even travelled as far as Dunkirk but at the last minute decided against the idea. This is confirmed in a letter of 28 June from Cardinal Fesch, an old friend of the family and Lucien's uncle, who wrote from Paris that Lucien had set out for London to get passports to move to America, and that Christine, who had recently arrived from England, would return in a few days (presumably to Rome).

July 1815. Throughout Great Britain there were huge celebrations at the victory over Napoleon. Dr Butler, who was away from Shrewsbury at the time, had a friend describe what it was like in the town when the local worthy and ex MP, Lord Hill, was the centre of attraction for their festivities: 'Our big days exceed all expectation. There could not be less than thirty thousand to forty thousand spectators to see Lord Hill enter the town. I conjecture the procession must have reached two miles foot and horse; no less than five thousand horses were in town; stalls and beds were at a great price. The dinner tickets sold for thirty shillings and upwards ... To drink tea in the Quarry there could not be less than twenty thousand to twenty-five thousand: immense tin canisters, capable of holding all your children, were the tea-pots; seven hundred pound weight of cake was cut up and distributed in baskets, with many barrels of ale. Near three thousand people were dined besides in the public houses, on good roast mutton, new potatoes, etc, etc, three pints of ale each and a paper of tobacco. There were no drunken people about, and all were satisfied with the dinner.'

Perhaps it was Alexandrine who decided that she would have her own celebrations on the safe return of Christine to the family. Although Lucien was absent she determined to mark the occasion by asking the artist Ingres to make a delightful sketch of the family (page 88/89). Another reason perhaps was that Alexandrine was again seven months pregnant in the July of 1815 and at 37 may have been feeling a little vulnerable and wanted to ensure that posterity would remember her family. Apparently she asked for Lucien to be included in the drawing but Ingres was unwilling to do so; the compromise was to include the statues in the background of Lucien and his mother, Letizia or Madame Mère as she was known.

Lucien Bonaparte had made the right decision not to return to England; he would not have been welcomed. His brother Joseph urged Lucien to follow him to America. Instead he vacillated not knowing what to do. Then the new Prime Minister, Fouché, ordered him to leave France. He headed for Grenoble but was arrested and taken to Turin where he had to persuade the Austrian Prime Minister, Metternich, that he should be allowed to return to Italy. Lucien finally arrived in Rome just as Alexandrine was producing her seventh child, his ninth child. The child was called Pierre.

2 November 1815. *The Times* reported: 'The Princess of Wales visited the Pope today, and was received with all the honours due to her rank. Her Royal Highness afterwards visited the Vatican, the Sculptor Canova, and Lucien Bonaparte, Prince of Canino. The Prince is preparing a brilliant fête for her Royal Highness.' This report would not have endeared Lucien to the Court in England as the Regent had been trying to divorce her.[114]

18 November 1815. Various reports noted that Lucien Bonaparte was in Rome and had permission to stay. Lucien still had the Villa Rufinella and the houses at Canino and Musignano to live in but at this time Rufinella was his favourite. It was a large house and the upkeep would have required a considerable income – which he did not have. Alexandrine must have made it very plain that they were going to require money. Perhaps even before he arrived home, she had made the point forcefully enough for Lucien to direct that another effort be made to sell the collection of paintings he had sent to England.

It was almost as if her pleas had been foreseen by Boyer, who was still in London , as on 20 November 1815 *The Morning Chronicle* posted the notice:

> LUCIEN BONAPARTE's Pictures. – The Amateurs of the Fine Arts are hereby informed, that the celebrated COLLECTION OF PICTURES belonging to Mr LUCIEN BONAPARTE, Prince of Canino, which was last year exhibited to the public, is now for SALE. Application may be made to the Chevalier Boyer, 31 Leicester Square, who will be ready to treat on reasonable terms with any persons disposed to purchase the whole collection, the merits of which are too well known to the public for any further description to be necessary.

This notice was repeated each week until the end of the year.

One could perhaps conclude from the repeated attempts to sell Lucien's pictures that Boyer had difficulty in doing so. To resolve the issue he would seem to have handed the problem to a Mr Stanley, at 29 St James Street, and asked him to sell the pictures at auction. Mr Stanley produced a *Catalogue of the Magnificent Gallery of Paintings, the property of Lucien Bonaparte, Prince of Canino,* and announced the sale for 14 May 1816.

Whether Lucien had abused his various official positions to amass a portable collection of disposable assets or had a genuine desire to collect well is open to debate. He did acquire paintings in dubious circumstances. Sir Richard Wolsey (1751-1805) had his collection pirated when it was on its way to England and several of his paintings appeared in Lucien's collection. There is little doubt that Lucien did have an educated eye and many of the paintings he collected then are now in the best galleries and museums around the world (some examples are on page 90).

In a later catalogue two paintings that belonged to the Lord Northbrook Collection were noted to have come from the Lucien collection: *The Guitar Player*, by Anthony Van Dyck, which was bought in 1816 for £84 and *Riposo*, ascribed to Murillo, which was also bought in 1816 for £80. Velazquez's *Lady with a Fan* (now in the Wallace Collection), and the *Drunken Silenus* from the Rubens studio were just some of the other paintings that had been included in Lucien's collection. Lucien appeared slow to understand the consequences of his decision to work again with his brother. The British perhaps saw his 'volte face', after years of promoting himself as a person who would not prostitute his principles, as something shameful and it is no wonder that neither pictures nor the poem sold well.

After Napoleon's final defeat and exile to St Helena the other members of the family, with the exception of Joseph in America, were confined to Rome and the Papal States. They now found themselves rather less welcome than before and were kept under surveillance. Lucien spent much of his time seeking peace and quiet at his Villa Rufinella, in Frascati and no doubt resumed his earlier interest in astronomy. He did not settle and was clearly contemplating a return to England when he wrote to Lord and Lady Holland 20 January 1816. He knew they were hugely supportive of Napoleon as he had met Lady Holland in Rome in 1814. Lucien wrote to her thanking her for a gift she had sent and asking for their help in obtaining passports for him and his family to return to England. After several exchanges of letters Lucien suggested that he might act as an intermediary between the Governments but Lord Holland replied later that he thought the idea not a good one as it might prejudice his cause and suggested that he should write direct to the Home Secretary (Lord Sidmouth).[115]

27 May 1816. We will recall that it is well over a year since we heard of any further progress on the purchasing of telescopes. Clearly the resumption of the war did not help. Perhaps Alexandrine had a view on the purchase. Lucien could by this time have expected some income from the art sale in London and

that may have prompted him to resurrect the scheme. In any case on this date William Herschel wrote to Chevalier Boyer, who is living at 31 Leicester Square, London, to ask him to come and inspect the 10 foot telescope which Lucien has ordered before it is packed for shipping to Italy and to translate the directions for its erection.

2 June 1816. William Herschel, responding to an unseen letter from Boyer understands he can expect Boyer on the 10th or 12th and assures him that 'I shall endeavor to have all necessary directions ready for your inspection'.

11 July 1816. Herschel informed Boyer that he will dispatch the telescope, by waggon in the following week. Boyer had also asked for details of the cases that Herschel had already delivered in August of 1815 to Barings which included the mirrors for both the 20 foot and 7 foot telescopes. Herschel then describes what he will send on this occasion. His description gives us a good idea of what a 10 foot telescope consisted of:

> A flat packing case 11 feet 6 inches long containing wood-work. A square case 11 feet long containing the tube; a flat case 9 feet 2 inches long containing woodwork. A case 5 feet 8 inches long containing iron work, and containing also two boxes; one with optical apparatus, and one with eye glasses etc. A heavy case 2 feet 6 1/2 inches square containing the great mirror and written instructions for erecting the telescopic apparatus.

Lucien's telescope would have looked similar to this wood cut image of a 20ft Herschel telescope. Image courtesy of The Royal Astronomical Society.

A week later Herschel informs Barings that the waggon should arrive into their 'care' by ' … Wednesday the 24th inst … about 3 or 4 o'clock … ' Herschel directs that the boxes 'must be kept dry and should be handled very carefully.' It is not known exactly when Lucien finally took possession of the telescopes but a letter dated February 1818, probably written by Père Maurice, but signed by Lucien, confirms that both parties are still discussing how best to use the telescope. This is the last letter on this subject.

Alexandrine produced two more children, a boy, Antoine in 1816, and Alexandrine-Marie in 1818. Their eldest daughter Charlotte finally married a man of her choice, Prince Mario Gabrielli, and all seemed well. Unfortunately their peaceful existence in the Frascati countryside was not to last for long. An unpleasant incident involving bandits attacking the house made the place feel unsafe and after two years they returned to Rome. In 1820 Napoleon died on St Helena. Lucien considered again going to America; brother Joseph, who was already there, even prepared for his arrival by renting a house for him in Philadelphia. However, the idea of emigrating was again discounted and the family moved to Bologna, still within the Papal States. Alexandrine, aged 45, produced her final child in 1823, another daughter, Constance.

We are told by some accounts that by 1825 Lucien, suffering under financial pressure, had 'retreated' to a smaller house in Senigallia, on the coast in the Marche region. He was still obtaining some income from the Canino estate but not enough to pay his debts. He borrowed from his uncle, Cardinal Fesch, and was only too happy to try and forget his troubles by immersing himself in the study of the stars – later claiming to have found some 20,000 using the same Herschel telescopes that he had bought in England. Alexandrine was left to manage the family and its affairs whilst her 50 year old husband followed his muse. She subsequently provided the catalyst for improving the family finances when she moved back to Canino without Lucien and realized that workers on the estate had found valuable Etruscan artefacts and were selling them. When Lucien eventually started to pay attention to the importance of his wife's activities – she was by now personally involved in excavating antiquities – he switched his enthusiasms to this new enterprise and started to organize excavations on an industrial scale. The income gained from the sales of the antiquities revived the family fortunes and Lucien could now indulge himself again and he resumed his enjoyment of the Canino estate.

Although Lucien made a small fortune from the excavations, posterity has also had some benefit, from the careful cataloguing that he insisted on and had published. Lucien's connection with this discovery of the ancient town of Vetulonia, or Vulci, will probably be his lasting memorial; for approaching nine tenths of all Etruscan pottery discovered to that date were found there.[116]

Some later commentators deplored the destruction of lesser objects and the lack of scientific approach to the dig but the cataloguing was done and objects were presented for public examination in a museum which Lucien established. These were important finds and many of the objects found are now in principal museums of the world, illustrating Etruscan and Greek culture.

Lucien's rural idyll was interrupted again by the politics of the time. Although he kept out of the plotting and scheming for power his sons were actively engaged. His brother Joseph, who was now head of the family, was tempted to return from America with hopes of regaining some influence and was urging the family to meet in England. Lucien wanted to continue writing and perhaps he considered that he could satisfy both his brother and his own desires if he joined Joseph there.

Joseph Bonaparte's arrival in London from America in 1832, and his subsequent rental of General Sir George Ashe's home at 23 Park Crescent, gave Lucien the confidence that he too might be welcomed. As a result, in April 1833, Lucien left Alexandrine to run the estate and the family and returned to England staying initially with Joseph but later he rented his own house in London. He not only wanted to write but he very much hoped to make some money from publishing his memoirs. As we have now come to expect Lucien was short of cash. He probably could not afford to bring his family to England but he did bring items to sell. Mssrs. Christies and Manson advertised the sale of 'a small but choice assemblage of painted greek pottery' from the 'collection of Lucien Bonaparte' just a month after his arrival. Informed by the provenance description in later auctions three of these vases are known to have found their way to Stowe, the home of the then Marquess of Chandos, later Duke of Buckingham. Again on 27 June 1833, Mr Phillips was auctioning a 'collection of antique bronzes dug up on the estate of Prince Lucien Bonaparte, from the tombs of the ancient Etruscan Kings.' They cannot have sold that well as the sale was repeated on 17 July.

Reportedly the Duke of Wellington called upon Lucien soon after his arrival in London and he returned the call by visiting Apsley House. By most accounts Lucien settled into the capital's social life easily. His daughter, Christine-Egypta, had married Lord Dudley Coutts Stuart (1803-1854) in July 1824, and they now lived in London. In consequence Lucien now had some good family connections from which he could benefit. Lord Dudley Stuart was the MP for Arundel at the time and Lucien would have welcomed the access this association would have given him to political thought at the centre of government. Both Lucien and Joseph began to turn to politics. The turmoil in Europe following the end of the Napoleonic Wars and the unhappiness of the French people with their Bourbon King, Charles X, encouraged Lucien to think he might promote the idea of a new style of republic. He was starting to think that he might be able to move back into French politics again. Others had their reservations. Louis Mailliard, Joseph's secretary, recorded in his diary comments that suggested his lack of respect for Lucien: 'everything Lucien says about France is not very brilliant'; 'Lucien is all imagination ... changing all the time', and ' ... he is a man who speaks well but who is of no use.' Lucien wrote a pamphlet, *De La République Consulaire ou Impériale*, in July 1833 and sent it to France and waited to see how it would be received. He wanted to return to France with some status. He was disappointed. It took until January 1834 for the French Chamber of Deputies to consider the idea and then dismiss it.[117]

On 28 June 1834, it was reported by *The Times* that on 7 June Lucien had attended a dinner of the Literary Society, as their guest of honour, at the Freemasons' Hall. In response to their toast to his health he gave the toast (in French):

> To the political principles, sacred treasure of the British constitution; to the inviolability of the private dwelling, to the independence of the jury, to the freedom of the press, and to the imprescriptible right of association! May these precious liberties, gentlemen, continue to constitute your happiness! But may they also cease to be foreign to France, who for forty years has been fighting to obtain them! ... and may all nations become as free as the hospitable people of Old England!

Lady Morgan's Memoire noted that on 3 August 1833 Lucien attended some entertainment at her London home and she mentioned that Lucien was lodging 'in a little bit of a house in Devonshire Street [No 50]. He and his brother have just enough to live on.'[118] Lucien is noted as visiting Lady Morgan again in 1835, 'for a sofa conversation'. Lucien has now been in England for two years. In all that time he had not returned to Italy or seen his wife and this despite her falling ill in the spring of 1835. What was keeping him in London?

Perhaps there were several reasons. Joseph's secretary, Mailliard, records that Joseph had to intervene to prevent a duel taking place between Lucien and another of Joseph's staff over Lucien's attentions to his wife. Lucien had started to write his memoires in 1835 and wanted them to be published in England as well as France. He apparently needed to stay in London to have them simultaneously translated into English as he wrote. He chose to have them translated by a woman, Anna Maria Gordon, who had been nanny to his two youngest daughters for some years in Rome. Alexandrine of course knew the woman and presumably trusted the pair to behave honourably but after years apart from Lucien it is not surprising that her letters make it plain that it is time he returned to Italy.

2 July 1835. It was announced that Mssrs. Foster was auctioning on behalf of Charles O'Neil, on 7 July 'Etruscan Vases and Urns of unusual size and beauty, from the collection of Lucien Bonaparte.'

6 May 1836. This note was announced in *The Times* as literary news from the *Metropolitan*: 'The Memoirs of Prince Lucien Bonaparte, written by himself, which have excited so much expectation, are about to be committed to the press ... '. Was the nation really holding its breath?

23 May 1836. Lucien may have read the following report in *The Times* with a sinking heart and perhaps before receiving any personal letter from Italy:

> Extract of a letter from Forli, in the Roman states, dated the 10th inst: - 'We have received, by letters from Rome, of the 6th inst, the following unfortunate details: - Two of the sons (Pierre and Antoine) of Lucien Bonaparte, Prince of Canino, carried away by the impetuosity of youth, killed a gamekeeper at Canino, in a hasty quarrel that arose between them. The Government immediately sent a detachment of Carabineers to arrest the young Princes, who resolutely resisted by force of arms, supported by other young men who joined them. On presenting the warrant of arrest, the lieutenant who commanded the party was killed by a pistol-shot from one of the Princes. A general contest ensued in which several were wounded and among them, it is said, a non-commissioned officer and two carabineers, very seriously. In the end the armed force gained the upper hand, and secured one of the Princes, but the other succeeded in effecting his escape. The brother who was secured was instantly sent to Rome under escort, and arrived a few moments after this deplorable event had been made known to the Government and to the elder brother, the Prince of Musignano [Charles-Lucien], who was quietly pursuing at Rome his favourite study of natural history. It is said the lieutenant who is killed was a relation of one of the prelates.

This shocking story relating to his own sons was still not enough to persuade Lucien that he ought to go home. Five days later *The Times* has reported that the Pope has ordered that the trial should be conducted with the greatest care. It also reported that Antoine who had escaped had fled out of the Papal States and into Tuscany. By June we learn that Pierre, the son who was in custody, has had a passport delivered for a foreign country and has been liberated from the Castle of St Angelo. His brother Antoine stayed in Tuscany and apparently forgotten turned his attentions to wine making.

13 August 1836. Back in England *The Metropolitan Magazine* announced that its next edition would contain 'exclusively copious and interesting extracts from the Prince Lucien Bonaparte's unpublished memoirs ... to prevent disappointment early orders should be given'.

27 September 1836. This day may well have brought disappointing news to Lucien as it was announced that the Duchess D'Abrantes' memoirs, *'MEMOIRS of NAPOLEON, his court and Family*, were now ready in 2 vols, handsomely bound and embellished with 16 portraits of the nearly complete Buonaparte family.' The Duchess had beaten him to it.

So concerned was Lucien to get his *Memoires* published that not even the death of his mother and the subsequent announcement in Rome that Letizia's executors needed the family to gather there for the opening of the will was enough to make Lucien return to Italy.

27 September 1836. *The Times* reported that Lucien's son (Pierre) had arrived at Portsmouth having sailed from New York on board the packet *St James*.

12 October 1836. *The Times* reported receiving the first volume of the Memoirs of Lucien Bonaparte, Prince of Canino. 'As the book is evidently a genuine production of the alleged writer, we shall take an early opportunity of noticing it.'

13 October 1836. *The Times*, carried an advertisement: 'We are requested to state that the Memoirs of Prince Lucien Bonaparte are now ready.'

By 29 October the newspaper reading public has started to form a view on Lucien's memoirs and they are writing letters to their editors. An article in *The Times* stated:

> We received at a late hour last night a manuscript copy (on tissue paper, such as police reports are written upon) of a letter of the Prince of Canino. It was so full of errors of transcription, that we fear we may in our translation have mistaken its meaning in one or two passages. We are surprised that this eminent foreigner should have thought it worth his while to answer the various hasty and ill-considered observations which one or two party prints (sic) have uttered against him. He should calmly wait the judgement of the public when it has had time to

read and digest his work. He will have to write a volume a week if he takes a pen to hand to refute the arguments.

The article then goes on to enumerate the complaints that Lucien has of his critics:

"It is made a subject of complaint that I do not recount sufficient anecdotes … I think it my duty to suppress all details unconnected with public affairs – of what use could they be? 2. I am accused of vanity because I speak of myself and my speeches … I am writing my own memoirs. 3. It was expected that more should have been said of Napoleon … 4. I have reserved for the last the most serious criticism – that which declares me at once to be an ultra-democrat and an ultra-Tory. Let me be here permitted to tell my judges that they have pronounced sentence as if they had not before them the documents connected with my trial." The Prince concludes his letter with some complimentary remarks on the *Examiner*, which while it combated his opinions had treated him with personal courtesy.

It would seem that following the disappointing reception of his *Memoirs* interest in Lucien faded rapidly and there are no further reports of either his activities or of the *Memoirs*. He decided to go home. There were no farewell parties this time and even his departure from London went unnoticed by the press except for a short announcement on 17 February 1838 which was taken from the Paris papers which reported 'The Prince of Canino (Lucien Bonaparte) arrived at Milan on the 2nd inst, on his way to Rome.'

After 5 years of absence Lucien rejoined Alexandrine at Senigallia. By 1840 Lucien had returned to Canino but it was not long before he fell sick and became gravely ill. Finding Canino too humid he attempted to move north to Siena but could only make the journey as far as Viterbo. After five days in agony, possibly from the same stomach cancer that killed his brother and sister, he died on 29 June 1840.

Once more Alexandrine was left to manage her family. She lived for fifteen more years and continued her writing with some success. It is recorded that in 1844 Alexandrine sold some sixty objects that had been found at Vulci, some from the 'Isis Tomb'. Most of the objects she sold have found their way into the British Museum. The distinctive bronze bust of a woman, shown overleaf, one of the objects she sold, is one of the earliest, 600BC, bronze objects to survive.

Somehow it seems a fitting end to the story that an object Lucien found as a result of Alexandrine's endeavours should now rest in England and particularly an object with the same enduring qualities as herself. If there is a hero to this tale it is probably she that is the heroine. Her own survival and that of most of her children are surely proof of her success.[119] She moved back to Senigallia and died there of cholera in 1855 aged 77. Her gravestone lies in the church at Canino.

* * *

This book started with a desire to discover the circumstances surrounding Lucien Bonaparte's residence in England. Unless and until a personal diary containing details of what Lucien might have termed 'domestic trivia' is discovered there is probably little more to find out about the family's stay in England. However, between the newspaper reports and the letters in the archives we can now be certain of the chronology of events. What else have we learned? It was surprising to find that after his imprisonment Lucien returned to England for such an extensive period but we have come to know that he was a man of many contradictions. A committed husband at first who later virtually abandons his family when one could argue they needed him most. He was a man who eschewed the trappings of office even when offered royal positions. He professed a dislike for all that Napoleon stood for only to rush to his side after his escape from Elba. He assumed the connoisseurship of the arts and collected avidly but only it would seem to realize the monetary value of the objects as soon as it became expedient. Perhaps his only lasting legacy will turn out to be his association with the Etruscan discoveries at Vulci.

Lucien's biographers have largely ignored his time in England apparently considering that it was of little consequence to him. Having now examined the records it seems likely that such an extended period of nearly four years was bound to have some effect on him and his family. His voluntary return to this country for a further five years is ample proof of a regard for England. Christine, his second eldest daughter, married an Englishman, Dudley Coutts Stuart. His son, Charles–Lucien, was deeply influenced by his time in England, and is quoted on his return as saying he felt it was like being in his 'native land'. As a noted ornithologist he became a member of the Linnean Society and visited London often to see people such as Edward Lear. Another daughter Laetitia married an Irishman, later Sir Thomas Wyse, but eventually lived with an English army captain. It would seem that in any examination of Lucien and his family members it would be quite wrong to ignore this English period in their lives.

Lucien's story of imprisonment has provided a unique window to some facets of life in late Georgian England. The correspondence between Colonel Leighton and the Foreign Office in particular demonstrating how government, despite the myriad concerns it had, retained the desire to acknowledge the needs of the individual. The degree to which the newspapers of the day took up the story and ran it for years on end was an unexpected discovery just as was their clear manipulation by both the government, Lucien, and members of the public. The ability to 'read between the lines', in 1812, would seem to have been a very necessary skill and one today that perhaps we would do well to emulate more often.

Lucien's perambulations around Ludlow and Worcester looking for a home have provided me with an extra strata of interest when examining a map or driving in my local area and recognizing a name or a place that he had visited. The same satisfaction came from finding Lucien's statue outside the church in Canino in which his family's mausoleum lies and where he and Alexandrine now lie together again. There can be no doubt that understanding our links with the past enhances our understanding of the present and that the pursuit of such knowledge can be turned into a very pleasurable occupation.

ACKNOWLEDGEMENTS

Should you find yourself in Rome I would recommend a visit to the Museo Napoleonico. It is a pleasure to visit as well as being hugely informative and instructive. I wish to thank the Director for granting me permission to use some delightful images and her staff for all the help they have given me. I would like to thank Marco Pupillo for his particular help and patience.

The Harvard Art Museum/Fogg Museum have generously allowed me to use the photograph of the *Portrait of the family of Lucien Bonaparte*, by Katya Kallsen, © President and Fellows of Harvard College. Without this image and that of the family on board HMS *President* provided by the Museo Napoleonico there would have been no book.

There have been many individuals who have helped and encouraged me in the production of this book but very special thanks are due to Julia Ionides, Gisèle Wall, my wife Janet and my daughter Joanna. The owners of both Dinham House and Thorngrove House generously gave me access to their properties and I am very grateful to them as well as to those who have allowed me to use images of their homes.

I would like to thank the staff at the archives and museums with whom I dealt: the National Archives - Kew, the Cambridge University Library, the Royal Astronomical Society, each of the Shropshire, Herefordshire and Worcester Archive/Record Offices, the Dudley Museum and the Ludlow Historical Research Group. The value of these institutions is immense and in a small acknowledgement to their dedication any profits from the production of this book will be given to two of my local charities, the Friends of Ludlow Museum and the Ludlow Civic Society.

Charles Bonaparte 1746-1785

Married:

Marie–Letizia 1750-1836

Joseph

1768-1844
King of Naples
and Spain

Married:
1. Julie Clary

1. Zénaïde
2. Charlotte

Napoleon

1769-1821
Napoleon I

Married:
1. Joséphine
2. Marie-Louise

1. 2. Napoleon-
Francois-Charles-
Joseph (Napoleon
II)

Lucien

**1775-1840
Prince of Canino**

Married:
**1. Christine
Boyer
2. Alexandrine de
Bleschamp**

**1.1. Charlotte
2. 1. Christine
3. Charles– Lucien
4. Letitia
5.Jeanne
6. Paul
7. Louis-Lucien
8. Pierre-Napoleon
9. Antoine
10. Alexandrine-Marie
11. Constance**

Eliza

1777-1820

Married:
1. Felix Bacciochi,
Prince of Lucca

Louis

1778-1846
King of Holland

Married:
1. Hortense de
Beauharnais

1.Napoleon-Louis
-Charles
2.Napoleon-Louis
3. Louis-
Napoleon,
Napoleon III

Marie–Pauline

1780-1825

Married:
1. Gen C.V.E.
Leclerc
2. Camille Borghese

Caroline

1782-1839

Married:
1. Joachim Murat

1.Napoleon-
Achille
2. Letizia
3. Lucien-
Napoleon-
Charles
4. Louise

Jerome

1784-1860
King of
Westphalia

Married:
1. Elizabeth Patterson
2. Catherine, Princess of
Würtemburg

1. 1. Jerome-Napoleon
-Bonaparte
2. Jerome-Napoleon-
Charles
3. Mathilde
4. Napoleon Joseph
Charles-Paul

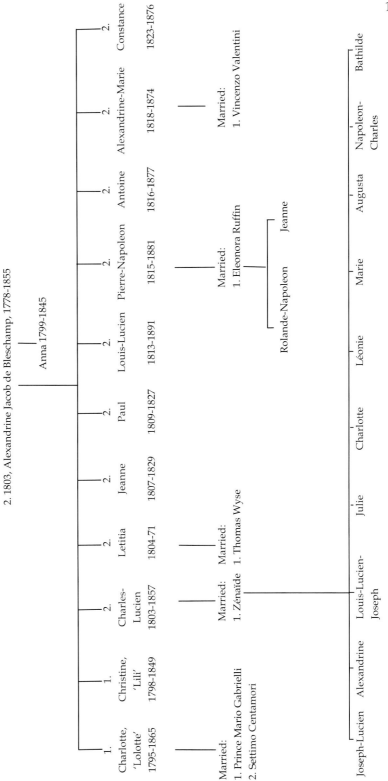

Lucien Bonaparte
1775-1840
Prince of Canino

Married:

1. 1794, Christine Boyer 1773-1800.

2. 1803, Alexandrine Jacob de Bleschamp, 1778-1855

Anna 1799-1845

Charlotte, 'Lolotte' 1795-1865 — 1.

Christine, 'Lili' 1798-1849 — 1.

Charles-Lucien 1803-1857 — 2.

Letitia 1804-71 — 2.

Jeanne 1807-1829 — 2.

Paul 1809-1827 — 2.

Louis-Lucien 1813-1891 — 2.

Pierre-Napoleon 1815-1881 — 2.

Antoine 1816-1877 — 2.

Alexandrine-Marie 1818-1874 — 2.

Constance 1823-1876 — 2.

Married:
1. Prince Mario Gabrielli
2. Settimo Centamori

Married:
1. Zénaïde

Married:
1. Thomas Wyse

Married:
1. Eleonora Ruffin

Married:
1. Vincenzo Valentini

Rolande-Napoleon

Jeanne

Joseph-Lucien   Alexandrine   Louis-Lucien-Joseph   Julie   Charlotte   Léonie   Marie   Augusta   Napoleon-Charles   Bathilde

NOTES

1. *Memoirs of the Private and Political life of Lucien Bonaparte* ... translated from the French, London, 1818, which were purported to be written by The Prince of Canino, these are shown as '*Memoirs*' in the text and secondly *Lucien Bonaparte et ses mémoirés* which were written by Theodore Lung, these are shown as '*ses Mémoires*'. The 1818 version would seem to contain several errors of fact and have to be treated with caution, the Lung version is probably a more accurate recollection based upon Lucien's own writing but is not a complete replication of Lucien's work as according to the authors of *Napoleon the Rebel* he omitted many pages of Lucien's original manuscript. Lucien was not interested in providing much detail of his private life and saw his memoirs principally as a record of his political speeches and thoughts. Lung had his own views on republicanism and his interpretation only adds to the misinformation.

2. The British Newspaper Archive.

3. The author has concluded that it is from Musignano that Lucien and family departed for America despite one memoire stating that he left *Tusculum*, Frascati, on 1st August. Musignano was their home at the time and the one which they returned to later. It made little sense to move the whole family to the other side of Rome a few days before setting out. Musignano is also much closer to the port of Civitavecchia. Lucien often headed his letters *Tusculum* and often when not actually there.

4. Tuscania lies to the south of the modern province of Tuscany.

5. Alexandrine Charlotte Louise Laurence Jacob de Bleschamp, b. 23 February 1778 Calais- d. 12 July 1855. Previously married to Gian Francesco Ippolito Jouberthon de Vamberthy who had died in debt at Port au Prince, Santo Domingo, in 1802. She married Lucien on 26 October 1803 in Charmant, Picardie having already born him a son, Charles-Lucien, in May 1803, after living as his mistress.

6. Count Charles de Châtillon, according to Stroud, a penniless artist.

7. Paul, b 19 February 1809.

8. Père Maurice, Abbé Maurice Malvestito (Atteridge). Padre Maurizio da Brescia (Fortunato Antonio Malvestiti) according to Stroud.

9. Anna Jouberthon, later Princess Herculani.

10. Filistine Charlotte Bonaparte,'Lolotte' b Saint Maximin 28 February 1795, to Christine Bonaparte, Née Boyer, d, 1865 Rome.

11. Christine-Egypta Bonaparte (nicknamed 'Lili', Atteridge) b, 18 October 1798 to Christine Bonaparte, Née Boyer, d 1847, Rome.

12. Christine Eléonore Bonaparte, Née Boyer, b 3 July 1771, married Lucien on 26 October 1803 in Saint Maximin, d 14 May 1800, Paris.

13. Atteridge, see Bibliography.

14. *The American Law Journal*, Volume 6. Page 21, edited by John Elihu Hall. Detail taken from the case study of a court case with regard to wages for the crew of the Hercules at Massachusetts District Court May 1811- Rand et al v the ship Hercules. The owner of the ship Nathaniel West had, on the eventual return of Hercules to America on 5 February 1811, tried to claim that as the voyage had made a loss he was not obliged to pay the crew. The court decided for the crew. This book is a Google ebook.

15. Murat had been made King of Naples in 1808, previously Marshall of France he had married Caroline Bonaparte, Napoleon's sister in 1800. She was a younger sister to Lucien born in Ajaccio, Corsica in 1782.

16. The size of the party at this stage of the journey varies according to the source, Stroud gives 46. Atteridge gives 40 which seems the more accurate when names are counted. As we see later the numbers dwindle.

17. Simonetta states 5 August. Atteridge says he embarked on the 7th and sailed that evening. The case notes in *The American Law Journal*, extracted from the ships log gives the date as departing on the 8th – which I favour. Stroud gives the departure date one day earlier on 7th. One explanation for the discrepancies is that the ship put to sea and embarked the family by cutter – see *Memoirs* page 37.

18. Mr Hill. *The Manchester Mercury*, 16 October 1810, identified MR Hill as The Honourable William Hill (1773-1842), MP for Shrewsbury (1796-1812). He was 3rd Baron Berwick from 1832. He lived, when at home, at Tern Hall which was later rebuilt and became Attingham, Shropshire.

19. Koslovski. Prince Pytor Borisovich (1783-1840). He was a diplomat, writer and linguist. He visited London 1812/1813 (when Lucien was at Thorngrove) and was well known in literary circles. He knew Madame de Stael, John Galt, Lord Byron, and Sir Walter Scott. He was according to Maria Edgeworth 'short, fat and good-humoured'.

20. HMS *Salsette*, a 5th rate frigate of 38 guns and built in Bombay she was the first Royal Navy ship built in teak.

21. Sir Robert Adair (1763-1855) had been sent to Constantinople in June 1808 by George Canning, Secretary of State for Foreign Affairs.

22. Memorandum on the Arrest of Lucien Bonaparte off Cagliari, in 1810. A confidential memorandum printed for the British Cabinet Office 7 December 1861. FO 881/1027. This document uses the word directed which seems a little odd as one might presume Sir Robert Adair outranked Mr Hill. It may have been the case that Sir Robert was in quarantine as well and therefore in a position to visit Lucien.

23. Ibid.

24.   Barrie, Robert (1774-1841). He ended his naval service as Rear Admiral; he was created Knight Commander of the Bath in 1840. He was a commissioner in Canada at Kingston and several place names are his legacy there, including the city of Barrie in Ontario.

25.   HMS Pomone, A 'fifth rate frigate commissioned in 1805. It was built by Brindley of Frinsburg, Kent. Amongst others the ship was credited with capturing a French Privateer in 1809 called the 'Lucien Charles' a victory no doubt the crew were quick to tell Lucien. This ship should not be mistaken for the French ship La Pomone that was captured by the British, HMS Arethusa, in 1794.

26.   The Prize was not just the value of the ship but the cargo as well. This reported largesse may well have been some journalistic notion romancing the British Navy ideal however Pomone had had more than the average success and perhaps the crew were actually happy to play the gentleman. It is more likely that they did not wish to upset their Captain.

27.   Described in George Percy Badger's book Description of Malta and Gozo, 1838. Frobert's Regiment according to Badger was a mercenary regiment hired by the British and raised by a French nobleman for Mediterranean service. The bargain was for a regiment of Greeks.   However, Frobert who was the Colonel, 'proceeded to gather together from the Levant, Archipelago and the continent a horde of various men, Greeks, Albanians, Sclavonians (sic), and what not, … equipped and transported to Malta … the officers were chiefly Germans … an English drill sergeant or two'.

28.   Napoleon had appointed Lucien as a Commissioner of War with the Army of the North.

29.   Cited by Eileen Holt, PRO, CO 158/16, Dispatch No 8 General Oakes dispatches to Sec of State.

30.   Description of Malta and Gozo, Badger.

31.   Lieutenant General Sir Hildebrand Oakes (1754-1822). His record shows him as very much the career soldier; His Service: North America 1775-1784 and prisoner of war 1781. Aide-de-Camp Ireland 1786, West Indies 1792. Service 1793-1815: Gibraltar 1792-1794, Aide-de-Camp and Quartermaster-General Corsica 1794-1796, Quartermaster-General Portugal 1796-1798, Brigade on Minorca 1798, Mediterranean 1800, Egypt 1801-1802 and wounded 1801, Brigadier on Malta 1802-1804.   Lieutenant Governor Portsmouth 1804,   Quartermaster-General Mediterranean 1806-1807. Commander-in-Chief Malta 1808-1810, Lieutenant General of the Ordnance 1814-1822. GCB 1820. Created a Baronet 1813. A further note from Lord Byron's Letters: Byron describes him as '..most accommodating of all possible chief magistrates' – he clearly facilitated meetings whilst on Malta, between Byron and Mrs Spencer-Smith, with whom he had then an 'everlasting Passion'.

32.   Wellesley, Marquess, Richard Colley (1760-1842). Elder brother of Arthur Wellesley, 1st Duke of Wellington. Governor General of India 1798-1805. Secretary of State for Foreign Affairs 1809-1812.

33. HMS *President* went via Cape of Good Hope to the East Indies and in 1811 took part in the capture of Java. After serving in the Irish Sea she was renamed the HMS *Piedmontaise* in 1815 but then was broken up in December of that year. The current HMS *President* is a shore establishment next to London Bridge.

34. Captain Samuel Warren RN was appointed to the Order of the Companion of The Bath, 4 June 1815 (*London Gazette*), by the Prince Regent on behalf of His Majesty George III. He was knighted in 1835.

35. Several dates are given for the arrival. Lucien's *ses Mémoires* state he arrived on 28 December 1810. *The Gentleman's Magazine* reports he landed on 18 December 1810. Atteridge has his arrival as the 12th. *The Morning Post* reported on 17 December that he arrived at Plymouth on Thursday 13 December. The ship's log ADM/51 2687 states the 13th.

36. *Salvador del Mundo,* This was originally a Spanish ship of 112 guns. Captured by the British in 1797 at The Battle of Cape St Vincent. In 1803 it was commissioned as the Port Admiral's ship at Plymouth and at the time of Lucien's arrival the Port Admiral was Sir Robert Calder (see Later Note). The ship was never made ready for active service at sea but was used to receive and train new recruits.

37. Barnpool is described even today as a beautiful anchorage, nestled under Mount Edgcumbe, which today is a country park, housing the National Camellia Collection.

38. *Morning Post* 22 December 1810.

39. *Morning Post* 19 December 1810.

40. Lymore Lodge and Deer Park, lay just a mile to the south east of the town of Montgomery. Principally built in 17th Century, it was a seat of Earl Powis in 1810. It was sold for demolition in 1931 and no longer exists. (See *Parks and Gardens UK*).

41. *Hampshire Chronicle* 14 January 1811.

42. See Abel in the bibliography.

43. George, Admiral Sir Rupert (1749-1823)

44. National Archives, the files in question are FO 881/1027, FO 27/84, 27/85, 27/89, 27/93, 27/110. These are mainly letter-books containing some 1643 pages in total.

45. *The Gentleman's Magazine.*

46. Sir Robert Calder (1745-1818) a naval officer since the age of fourteen. He had a distinguished career that ended badly for him - he attended a court-martial, at his own request, to clear his name in 1805. He was reprimanded for not pressing home an attack on the French but acquitted of cowardice and disaffection. In 1810 he had just been promoted Admiral and appointed Commander in Chief Plymouth. He was appointed Knight Commander of the Bath in 1815.

47. Lieutenant General Richard England (1755 -1812) Governor of Plymouth at the time. He was from an Irish family of Lifford, Co. Clare. He fought in the

were sent through wire set up alongside the developing rail networks. By 1852, 4000 miles of wire were in use in UK.

64. In Lucien's *Memoire*, the name Twinam is given. The only reference to this name is of a man at Plymouth and I am confident it is an error and that Dickinson is the correct individual – FO 27/84 dated 1 March 1811.

65. Butler, page 79.

66. *Hereford Journal* 23 November 1814.

67. This is Lieutenant Colonel Francis Knyvett Leighton, (1772-1835), Educated Shrewsbury School and Rugby. He entered the army as an ensign, aged 17, in the 46th Regiment, commanded by his relative Sir Baldwin Leighton. He moved to the 61st Regiment of Foot. He saw service in Gibraltar, St Lucia, Egypt and the Red Sea. He retired from regular service and joined the Shrewsbury Volunteers. He married Louisa, daughter of St Leger St Leger, 1st Viscount Doneraile. He died aged 63 of a heart attack in Shrewsbury whilst out riding with his daughter. *Gentleman's Magazine* Volume 157 Page 95, Obituary.

68. Baring, Alexander. The Barings brothers were instrumental in facilitating the purchase of Louisiana by America in 1802. This sale helped Napoleon a great deal to finance the war against Britain.

69. Shrewsbury Record Office, 6683/4/344.

70. *The Hereford Journal* 27 February 1811.

71. Robert Southey (1774-1843), an English 'Romantic' poet. Taken from *The Life and Correspondence of Robert Southey*, page 310.

72. Taken from *The Arkwrights: Spinners of Fortune* by RS Fitton, 1989. page 233.

73. Colonel Eyton, this is probably the father of Col Philip Eyton who lived at Whitton Cottages, Leintwardine and was a member of the Leintwardine Fishing Club. (See by the same author *Fishing in Time: The History of the Leintwardine Fishing Club*, Stonebrook Publishing, 2011).

74. Mawley – Rev Robinson had been mistaken on two counts, the house is Mawley Hall, not Morley, near Cleobury Mortimer, Shropshire, and was owned by Sir Walter Blount, not Blunt. The Blunts lived in Southern England.

75. *Memoirs*, page 64.

76. P & H Le Mesurier, further detail of the bank failure lie in the Jersey Archive.

77. Hanbury-Tracy, Charles (1778-1858) became Baron Sudeley in 1838. He did eventually sell the Morville estate in 1814.

78. *Hoggs Weekly Instructor* Volume 5, 1847.

79. See Atteridge, page 265.

80. This is John Lagier Lamotte who is noted in *A List of Parish Registers and other Genealogical Works*, ed. by Frederick Arthur Crisp. Published 1897 by Private press of F. A. Crisp, London, and as being at Thorngrove in 1812 (and so is in error as we know that Lucien was there then).

81. *Measuring Worth*, Lawrence H. Officer and Samuel H. Williamson, '*Purchasing Power of Money in the United States from 1774 to 2010,'* Measuring Worth, 2011. Measuringworth.com. All the sums within the text have been con-

verted using this means and in relation to the Retail Price Index.

82. A pier (mirror) or pier glass often referred to as hanging between two windows.

83. Some references suggest that Lucien's collection of artefacts were shown in Ludlow at Dinham and were the forerunner of the Ludlow Museum. There is nothing to substantiate this idea, however, it is not unreasonable to suppose that guests invited to see the collection were prompted into action, such as Thomas Andrew Knight who became a founder member of the Ludlow Museum.

84. Coventry, Lord (1758-1831), George William, 7th Earl of Coventry, Lord Lieutenant of Worcestershire 1808-1831, Colonel of the Worcestershire Militia. He lived at Croome Court, south of Worcester at this time. The letter is in Worcester Archives 3261 705/73.

85. *Life of Sir Walter Scott*, JG Lockhart, page 351.

86. Miller, William RB, 1769-1844, prominent publisher of his time at 50 Albemarle Street, London.

87. Butler, Doctor Samuel, 1774-1839, b Kenilworth, Rugby School, St John's College Cambridge, Latin and Greek scholar, BA 1796, MA 1799, 1798 Headmaster Shrewsbury School, whilst still Headmaster appointed to clergy at Kenilworth 1802, Lichfield 1807, acquired Doctorate of Divinity 1811, 1836 became Bishop of Lichfield. He taught Charles Darwin who did not like his time at the school as it was 'strictly classical'.

88. Bibliography 11.

89. *Letters and Journals of Lord Byron*, page 315.

90. Morlaix, Brittany, France.

91. See Abel, page 118.

92. Ibid.

93. See Atteridge, page 270.

94. Butler, page 78.

95. Russell, Jonathan. Appointed US Chargé d' Affaires 27 July 1811-29 July 1812

96. Charles Babbage, 1791- 1871, FRS, mathematician, philosopher and inventor, 'father of the computer'.

97. *Charles Babbage, letters: Pioneer of the Computer*, by Anthony Hyman, Princeton University Press, 1982.

98. From: *A Publisher and his Friends: Memoir and Correspondence from the late John Murray,* by Samuel Smiles, Minerva Group, 2003. Murray, John 1778-1843, bought Miller's publishing business in 1812 when Miller retired at the early age of 42.

99. Tax information thanks to *The Regency Redingote*, website.

100. Madame de Laborde, Thérésa. An interesting woman. Using here a name of a past husband, she had many. She was one of the leading socialites in Paris. By this time she was married to Comte de Caraman and was known as Princess Chimay.

American Wars and was wounded three times. He was a very tall man, reputed-ly 6ft 6inches, who was nicknamed 'Great Britain'. He served in Canada. He was promoted to Lieutenant General in 1803. He was Colonel of 5th Foot (Northumberland Regiment) 1801-1812. His son Richard was also a soldier who went on to command a division in the Crimean War.

48. Lord Boringdon (1772-1840), John Parker, later from 1815 Earl of Morley, He lived at Saltram and was an active member of the House of Lords. He was a fellow of the Royal Society.

49. The Kings Arms Hotel still exists.

50. *Redding: Fifty Years' Recollections.* Cyrus Redding, Skeet 1858.

51. Saltram is now in the hands of the National Trust.

52. Hamilton, William Richard (1777-1859) FRS, archaeologist, traveller and diplomat. Involved in the securing of the Rosetta stone, 1801. He was secretary to the African Association at the same time that Sir Joseph Banks was associated with it. After his spell at the Foreign Office 1809-1822 he was Minister at the Kingdom of Two Sicily's at Naples. He succeeded Sir Thomas Lawrence as Secretary of the Society of Dilettanti. He was later a trustee of the British Museum. He was a founder of The Royal Geographical Society and became its president.

53. *Morning Post* Tuesday 25 December 1810.

54. *Ipswich Journal* 29 December 1810.

55. *Morning Chronicle* 27 December 1810 A report dated 24 December.

56. Chudleigh is a market town, near the River Teign, 9½ miles South of Exeter, then containing 2278 inhabitants (according to the census of 1831).

57. As reported in *The Cheltenham Chronicle* 3 January 1811.

58. *The Morning Post* 31 December 1810. *Hereford Journal* 2 January 1811 *Manchester Mercury* 15 January 1811.

59. Stone House, Onibury, was demolished to make way for the present Stokesay Court.

60. Walcot, near Lydbury North, Shropshire was purchased by the Clive family in 1764.

61. *En bon point* – stout.

62. Richard Payne Knight (1750-1824) 'connoisseur', collector, numismatist and scholar. He had, in 1780, completed building Downton Castle. A building and 'picturesque' parkland which was fast attracting visitors. The castle at this time was occupied by Knight's brother Thomas Andrew Knight who in his own right was becoming well known for his horticultural activities. Other visitors to Downton came for the fishing in the river Teme – Sir Humphry Davy being one enthusiast.

63. Telegraph, A French Engineer, Claude Chappe, invented the semaphore system which was copied by the Admiralty for communicating from London to the Navy Ports and was in position in 1810. It was 1838 before electric impulses

101. Louis Lucien Bonaparte, *The peerage.com*. and the *Shropshire Roman Catholic Registers.*

102. Sir Edward Blount, 8th Baronet of Sodington, Worcs.

103. Moore, Thomas, 1779-1852, Irish poet, singer and songwriter. A friend of Byron's who was responsible with Jon Murray for burning Byron's memoirs after Byron's death.

104. Tasso. Torquato Tasso was an Italian poet of the 16th Century.

105. The letter is found in *Memoirs of Rev F Hodgson*, page 279.

106. De Stael, Madame, Germaine de Stael, 1776-1817, French Swiss woman of letters who epitomized the women of culture in Europe. Writer and poet. She was not so well received by the English. This information from the *Memoirs of John Murray*, Ch XIII.

107. Rouw, Peter, the younger, 1771-1852. A successful wax modeller appointed as Modeller of Gems and Cameos to the Prince Regent. He lived in London.

108. Chessher, Robert (1750-1831), DNB. He was considered by some the pioneer of English orthopaedics. He was noted for his work on curvatures of the spine and correcting limb deformities. He lived in Castle Street, Hinckley, Leicestershire and is buried in St Mary's church where there is a large memorial to him.

109. The Complete Guide to the Herschel Objects. See bibliography.

110. William Herschel papers in the Royal Astronomical Society collection. Royal Greenwich Observatory, MS.RGO 35/170/12/1/4, now held in the Cambridge University Library.

111. The Georgian Planet (*Georgium Sidus*). Sir Joseph Banks and others per-suaded Herschel to name his discovery of Uranus in 1781 as the Georgian Planet in the hope of obtaining the favour of the King and thereby allow Herschel to pursue astronomy full time. The planet remained so called until after Herschel's death when the name was changed to fit in with the nomenclature of the other planets named after ancient gods.

112. The 'Pope' of Holland House: Selections from the correspondence of John Wishaw and his Friends 1813-1840, Wishaw J , London , 1906.

113. *Charlemagne: or the Church Delivered* … can be read online.

114. Princess of Wales, this was Caroline of Brunswick, married to the Prince of Wales in 1795. After the birth of their child Princess Charlotte, the couple sepa-rated. Once he became Regent and as George IV he continued to seek a means of divorcing Caroline. She left England for Italy in 1814. She returned in 1820 when George IV's coronation but was barred from it and died shortly afterwards in 1821.

115. Keppel, Sonia, *The Sovereign Lady*, quoting from the Holland House (Napoleonic) Papers, MSS 51525-9.

116. Dennis, George, *The Cities and Cemeteries of Etruria*, London, J Murray 1848.

117. The manuscript is held at the Library of Yale University.

118. Lady Sydney Morgan (née Owenson) (1778c-1859). Anglo-Irish novelist and socialite, author of *The Wild Irish Girl* (1860).

119 The Children: How the children fared:

Charlotte (1795-1865) married Prince Mario Gabrielli (1773-1841)

Christine (1798-1847) married Lord Dudley Coutts Stuart (1803-1854) in July 1824 and lived in England.

Anna (1795-1845) she married Alfonso Hercolani of Blumberg and became Countess Hercolani and later secondly Princess Maurice Jablonowski.

Charles-Lucien (1803-1857) married Zénaïde, and moved to America to join his Uncle Joseph. He developed an interest in ornithology and collaborated with JJ Audubon. He returned to Europe in 1828. His story as a renowned naturalist is told by Patricia Tyson Stroud in *The Emperor of Nature, 2000*. Zénaïde produced twelve children.

Letizia (1804-1871) married in 1821, Sir (1857) Thomas Wyse (1791-1862), educated Trinity College, Dublin. They lived at Viterbo following their marriage but moved to Waterford, Ireland, on inheriting the estate in 1825. Despite producing two sons the marriage did not work, she was even confined to a convent at one stage, and they agreed to separate in 1828. She had three further children with Captain John Hodgson. Thomas Wyse became a British Minister to Greece, was made A KCB for his efforts and died in Athens.

Jeanne (1807-1829/8) married Marquis Honoré Honorati (1800-1856) but died shortly afterwards.

Paul (1809-1827), when 18 ran off to join the Greeks fighting against the Turks. He became a low ranking officer on a British frigate *Hellas* commanded by Lord Cochrane but died of wounds after accidently shooting himself.

Louis-Lucien (1813-1891) born in England at Thorngrove became a linguist and from 1850 onwards lived in London and worked on many linguistic projects. He eventually retired on a British pension.

Pierre-Napoleon (1815-1881) married Justine Ruffin (1832-1905). He became something of an embarrassment to the wider family and earned the nickname the 'Wild Boar of Corsica'. Always violent he eventually killed a man and was due to be executed but was reprieved after Papal intervention and exiled.

Antoine (1816-1877) settled in Italy as a winegrower.

Alexandrine-Marie (1818-1874) married against her mother's wishes as a teenager one Valentini di Laviano.

Constance (1823-1876) became the abbess of Convent du Sacré-Coeur, Rome.

BIBLIOGRAPHY

1.   Abel, Francis, *Prisoners of War in Britain 1756-1815*, Oxford University Press, 1914.(Available on Internet Archive, (IA).

2. Atteridge, Andrew Hilliard, *Napoleon's Brothers*, Methuen,1909. (IA).

3. Badger, George Percy, *Description of Malta and Gozo,* 1838. (IA).

4.   Bonaparte, Lucien, *Memoirs of the Private and Political Life of LUCIEN BO NAPARTE, Prince of Canino,* translated from the French in two volumes, H Colburn, 1818. (IA).

5.   Bonaparte, Lucien, *Charlemagne; ou, L'église délivrée; poème épique, en vingt-quatre chants.* 2 volumes (London: Longman, Hurst, Rees, Orme, and Brown, 1814).

6. Bonaparte, Lucien, *Lucien Bonaparte et ses Mémoires, 1775-1840.* Theodore Lung, 1882.

7.   Bratton, Mark. *The Complete Guide to the Herschel Objects*, Cambridge University Press, 2011.

8.   Bulmer, *Catalogue of the splendid collection of pictures belonging to prince LUCIEN BONAPARTE, which will be exhibited for sale by private contract, on monday the sixt day of February, 1815, and following days, at the New Gallery, Bulmer 1815.*

9.   Butler, Samuel, grandson to , *The Life and Letters of Dr Samuel Butler,* Head-master of Shrewsbury School 1798-1836, and afterwards Bishop of Lichfield. J Murray, 1896.

10. Byron's Letters and Journals: *Famous in my Time*, 1810-1812.

11.   Dennis, George, *The Cities and Cemeteries of Etruria*, London, J Murray 1848.

12.   Fitton, RS , *The Arkwrights: Spinners of Fortune*, Manchester University Press, 1989.

13.   Holt, Eileen, *The Exile of Lucien Bonaparte 1810-1814*.   Includes material from a translation of *L'Exil de Lucien Bonaparte* from *Revue de L'Institute Napoleon*, No 141, (1983), Paris pp25-51. by Eileen Holt.

14.   Junot, The Duchess D'Abrantes (Madame Junot), *Memoirs of Napoleon, His Court and Family*, R Bentley, 1836.

15.   Keppel, Sonia, *The Sovereign Lady*, Hamish Hamilton, 1974

16.   Simonetta & Arikha, *Napoleon and the Rebel*, Palgrave Macmillan, 2011.

17.   Southey, Rev Charles, son of, Robert Southey, *The Life and Correspondence of Robert* Southey, London ,1849.

18.   Stroud, Patricia Tyson, 2000, *The Emperor of Nature*, University of Pennsylvania Press.

INDEX